MW01042535

PRAISE FOR *BUILDING BLOCKS OF PERSONALITY TYPE*

"This book takes the usual personality type charts and descriptions and makes them personal through the use of meaningful examples and language tailored to the individual. The creative use of vignettes, gifts, and contributions by type is a refreshing new way to look at material that can seem otherwise daunting. Thumbs up!"

—Tom E. Dailey, President, Valtegrics

"This book is a groundbreaking work conveying the complexity of the eight-process model of type with clarity and precision. With an abundance of clarifying quotes and vignettes, it grounds the theory and provides a versatile tool for personal development."

—Shoya Zichy, author, *Women and the Leadership Q: The Breakthrough System for Achieving Power and Influence*

"Leona Haas led a seminar some years ago which profoundly deepened my understanding of how individual preferences play out in people. I have applied that learning in leading the governing boards of a NYSE Corporation, an elite private college as well as a number of private firms in which I have invested. Now Leona and coauthor Mark Hunziker have put it in a book. Bravo. An even more efficient means to learn invaluable lessons for leading and managing people in organizations."

—Nordahl L. Brue, Lawyer/Entrepeneur

"*Building Blocks of Personality Type* offers its readers a depth of understanding about personality theory that is truly unique among books of its kind. It provides the most comprehensive and accessible descriptions of the 'eight intelligences' that I have ever seen, and I look forward to relying on this resource for years to come."

—Don Kjelleren, Vice President, Vermont Association of Psychological Type

BUILDING BLOCKS
OF PERSONALITY
TYPE

A Guide to Discovering the
Hidden Secrets of the Personality Type Code

LEONA HAAS
MARK HUNZIKER

TypeLabs
27636 Ynez Road L-7 #346
Temecula CA 92591
http://www.typelabs.com

Myers-Briggs Type Indicator, *MBTI*, and *Myers-Briggs* are trademarks or registered trademarks of the Myers-Briggs Type Indicator Trust in the United States and other countries.

Printed in the United States of America

Library of Congress Control Number: 2011934070

ISBN: 978-0-9833657-1-6

This book is dedicated by Leona and Mark to

Carl G. Jung, for his relentless courage in
exploring the daunting mysteries of the psyche.

Isabel Briggs Myers, for her tireless and loving
dedication to helping humankind.

Katharine D. Myers, for her grace, caring,
and quiet devotion to Isabel and the purpose of the MBTI®.

Daryl Sharp, for his profound
understanding and clarity.

John Beebe, for his powerful insights and
remarkable patience in sharing them.

Mary Thompson, for her wise counsel.

by Leona to

Stanislaus and Agnes Nowicki, for all their
sacrifices and the gift of life.

Richard Haas, for his unconditional
love and belief in me.

Dawn Haas Bowders, for her ideas, technical
expertise, and continuous help.

Dana Balaz, my ENFP daughter, for helping me
understand and value opposing personalities.

Cheyenne and Alexandra Balaz, for their hugs
and kisses when I really need them.

Anthony Harley Nowicki, for teaching me to see type
through the eyes of a child.

Margaret and Gary Hartzler, for their true dedication,
caring, and sharing of knowledge.

All my workshop and Qualifying Program participants, for their
honest sharing of themselves to make this book happen.

and by Mark to

Robert J. Hunziker, for his love and
often underappreciated wisdom.

ISTJ

Optimistic

Si	Hero
Te	Parent
Fi	Child
Ne	Aspiriational/Inferior

Shadow ESTP

Pessimistic

Se	Nemesis
Ti	Critic
*Fe	Trickster
Ni	Demon

CONTENTS

PART ONE
AN INTRODUCTION TO THE
EIGHT-PROCESS MODEL OF TYPE

PART TWO
THE EIGHT JUNGIAN MENTAL PROCESSES

PART THREE
BEYOND PROCESS WATCHING

APPENDICES

Building Blocks of Personality Type belongs on the shelf of everyone interested in understanding and making use of Jungian psychological type and the Myers-Briggs Type Indicator® (MBTI®) assessment in their own lives and/or in helping others. It is to be read and used often as a valuable reference.

The authors have succeeded in conveying the full complexity of the eight-process model of type and its application in a manner that is clear and accessible to the professional and interested layperson alike. It is wonderfully user friendly. As I read it, I felt that the authors were sitting with me and I was the "you" they were addressing.

Leona's years of work with the government when she was working across the range of government hierarchy in terms of education, level of jobs, and experience, have served her well in presenting information in a manner that speaks across the spectrum. My first experience in observing her workshop was with a group of employees totally unsophisticated in anything psychological—they understood and responded with enthusiasm.

The collaboration between the two authors began at a workshop on the eight mental functions led by Leona Haas. Mark Hunziker was a participant. Mark wanted to learn more. Leona wanted to record a complete description of her model but her forte was live presentation, not writing. An hour's conversation later, the joint project was launched. Mark would provide his writing and structuring skills and gain the opportunity to study the eight-process model up close. Leona would be able to make her work available to a wider audience. "Two introverted intuiting types do not need much information or time to know when something 'fits'!"

Building Blocks of Personality Type demonstrates the success of this "fit." The writing is clear and coherent. Complex ideas are explained with precision, simplicity, and accuracy. The organization of the book takes an overwhelming amount of knowledge and presents it in a logical structure that makes the content accessible to the reader.

The development of the eight-process model of type is a giant step in understanding and using Jungian psychological type and the MBTI® assessment.

Leona Haas has been instrumental in developing and instructing others in the eight-process model of type. This model enables in-depth understanding of the eight mental processes that form the core of Jungian type theory, and it also provides a new and enriched model of feedback.

Katharine C. Briggs's major contribution was her profound understanding of Jungian theory and her recognition of psychological type as an invaluable model of development in healthy personalities. Her daughter Isabel Briggs Myers's major contribution was her pioneering work in creating the sixteen type model with its four-letter code as a way of giving individuals access to their Jungian preference type. For many years, interpretation focused on the four dichotomies, E-I, S-N, T-F, and J-P, although Myers had used her understanding of the eight processes in her naming of each type (for example, ESTJ as an extraverted thinking type with introverted sensing). The only description of these eight processes was a four-page summary compiled by Myers in *Gifts Differing*.

Most practitioners are introduced to Jungian ideas when they begin to use the MBTI®; however, over the years their understanding has gradually moved from basic type through type dynamics, type development, and on to Jung's model of the psyche and his life-long development model of Individuation. As practitioners gradually deepened their knowledge, attention was turned to the need for understanding more fully these four functions in both attitudes, that is, the eight mental processes.

Leona was among the leaders in recognizing this need. She has devoted herself with introverted intuitive intensity to learning more through constant questioning of individuals of different types, consultation with experts, and reading. Her treasury of knowledge, contained in this book, is the outcome.

Her seamless integration of the eight processes into the complex whole of the Jungian system of personality is a valuable bonus gift to the reader.

Historically, the knowledge of our "four letters" has given many individuals and groups important insights in self-understanding/self-acceptance and in the understanding and appreciation of others who are different from themselves. However, those of us who have journeyed further have found a richness of understanding and a perspective that enhances our lives immeasurably. This book provides the door to that richness. Welcome!

Katharine D. Myers
The Myers-Briggs® Trust

The word mental, meaning "of or pertaining to the mind," has too often been used to suggest abnormality. Robert Graves and Joseph Campbell have warned us that myth is a word we use to refer to "other people's religion." Likewise, mental is the word we use to refer to other people's ways of using their minds. Leona Haas and Mark Hunziker have dignified these sidelong looks we give one another by identifying what we are observing as "mental processes" found in everybody, the only differences being which processes we each give emphasis to and in which order.

In this endeavor, they follow the work of the Swiss psychiatrist C. G. Jung, who, in the first part of the twentieth century, influenced by psychologists in French-speaking Switzerland and France, began to engage himself with the typical differences in human consciousness. One of these mentors was Alfred Binet, for whom consciousness was "intelligence." Binet sought to measure intelligence, and our most commonly used "intelligence test" is still called the "Stanford-Binet." By 1902, when Jung was studying in Paris, Binet had noticed, even in his own daughters, dramatic differences in learning styles, to which he gave the names "externospection" and "introspection." Within a decade, Jung had introduced his own notion of a "turn" of mind into the terms for the basic mental attitudes by calling them "Extraversion" (outward turning) and "Introversion" (inward turning). A further decade enabled Jung to differentiate various functions of consciousness, four in all, through which these basic attitudes of mind could be expressed in dramatically different ways. His descriptions of thinking, feeling, sensation, and intuition as expressed in both the extraverted and introverted attitudes form the heart of his book *Psychological Types* (1921). This classic became an inspiration to Isabel Briggs Myers in the 1940s, as it had been a generation earlier to her mother, Katharine Briggs. It led them to develop together a practical instrument for capturing the differences in the ways individuals use their minds in all the settings of their lives—the Myers-Briggs Type Indicator®, which has become the most widely used instrument for identifying normal personality differences in America today.

Psychological Types was the basic inspiration for the eight-function model that, as a Jungian analyst inspired by such clinical teachers as Marie-Louise von Franz, Jo Wheelwright, and Wayne Detloff, I brought to practitioners of type assessment in the 1980s. Leona Haas was among the very first type consultants (alongside Kathy Myers and Margaret and Gary Hartzler) to grasp what I was getting at: that the normal mind cannot be adequately described with a four-function model of its processes, even if the two attitudes of Extraversion and Introversion are somehow included to explain some of the differences between the ways different functions are expressed by different people. Subsequently, thanks as much to Haas's teaching as my own, a number of others have come aboard. She has recognized that we cannot be literate in the ways of the mind without a clear, individualized sense of what all eight mental processes look like and of how they are experienced by the actual persons using them.

It is a pleasure to have her book to recommend to those who have come to my own lectures and asked me to give more extended and systematic descriptions of the eight function-attitudes (to use the helpful term that Dick Thompson introduced a few years ago). She has made the most practical use possible of my analytic interpretation of Jung's visionary theory. Haas has succeeded in taking the eight function-attitude model, in all its complexity, into workaday corporate settings, where it has instantly proved its power to unlock the understanding of serious impasses and to significantly improve the integrity of a business's team building.

That is not the extent of this model's potential application, however. In this book, elegantly realized with the patient assistance of Mark Hunziker, himself a formidable student of the mind, Leona Haas has managed to produce the most practically detailed and psychologically accurate orientation to the eight processes that I have seen. I heartily recommend it to the beginner as well as to anyone who imagines he or she is already adept in this field. The truth is, we all have a great deal to learn about the building blocks out of which our "minds" are made. In my own efforts to master the architecture of such a wondrous structure, I expect to be reading this book for many years to come.

John Beebe

Over the past half-century, many millions of people around the world have been aided in their personal and professional development through a model of personality that was developed by Carl Jung, Katharine Briggs, and Isabel Briggs Myers. The Myers-Briggs Type Indicator® (MBTI®) provides both the framework and the main tool for the model of what has come to be known as personality type, or just type for short. *Building Blocks of Personality Type* is an attempt to begin a comprehensive description of a certain way of thinking about type and the benefits that this approach offers.

We feel the need to give this view of type theory a label, the "eight-process model of type," in order to distinguish this paradigm from some misconceptions that have grown up around the MBTI® personality inventory and personality type. Although we call it a model, we are not talking about anything new or separate from the framework of the model that has served so well for all these years. We are, in fact, simply attempting to help clarify the core of the theory that was developed by Jung, Briggs, and Myers and to integrate subsequent work that has built directly upon that foundation.

Many type professionals will find that we are describing how they already think about type. We believe that these folks will, nonetheless, find useful and illuminating nuggets in the pages that follow. They may gain insights from the descriptions of the mental processes, or perhaps get some new ideas about how the model can be applied, or possibly learn something new about how the different aspects of the model mesh to produce the "dynamics" of type.

Others who work with type may find that eight-process type represents a dramatic and difficult shift in their understanding. In many of

Leona's advanced workshops, attendees find themselves going through a bit of a paradigm shift. Usually she hears from these people, after they have had time to digest the new information, that they can never go to back to the way they worked with type before. If you find that the eight-process model challenges some of your assumptions and practices, we urge you to bear with us. We are convinced that the theoretical model and practical descriptions that follow are at the heart of the most effective practices in use today, and that they are particularly helpful in teaching the basics of type through feedback and verification, as well as for delving more deeply into the important insights of Jung's theory of personality.

Our main focus in this work is on describing Jung's mental processes as completely and vividly as possible, as you will actually *experience* them. This is not only the first step in the eight-process approach to type but also a rewarding experience in itself. By looking at personality through process watching, you are likely to learn things that will change your perspective from this point forward, regardless of whether you are an experienced professional or you have never even heard of personality type. Through simple descriptions of the four different ways that we take in information and the four different ways we make decisions, you will learn to value your own gifts more highly. You will also begin to better understand and appreciate the perspectives of those around you. Conflict management, decision making, communication, management of change and transition, exploration of your teaching and learning styles and those of your children, career choices, and daily life will all be easier and more positive and will actually become opportunities for enriching your life!

We confess to also having a hidden agenda. We are out to save the world. It is tremendously rewarding for us to watch individuals, teams, and organizations grow as a result of exposure to this expanded approach to personality type. That is the immediate, day-to-day gratification of our work. But we are energized on another level too: by the conviction that a better appreciation of psychological type and how it influences relationships and interactions could be a vital key to unlocking the human potential that is needed in order to learn how to live together on this planet. This belief was a driving force behind Isabel Myers's amazing contributions as well. We believe, as she did, that animosity and bloodshed are but reflections of the immature and frightening shadow side of our own personalities. We also believe that the path to an exciting new maturity level in human evolution—a path of enhanced cooperation, collaboration, and coexistence—lies through the psychic development that Jung called "individuation."

Albert Einstein pointed out that we cannot expect to resolve complex problems from within the same mindset that created them. Margaret Wheatley, throughout her lectures and writings, has made a convincing argument that relationships, information flow, and self-definition are the ultimate determinants of how human beings interact. The state of consciousness from which we approach these critical human activities may very well be the key factor in determining the success or failure of all human systems: families, teams, communities, corporations, and even nations.

Regardless of one's personal motivation for exploring the mental processes, the inevitable result of doing so is an elevation of our level of awareness. The potential consequences of such a shift in consciousness are dramatic—for individuals, for family, for social and work groups and, by extension, for the entire human community. By enhancing our understanding of the eight mental processes, we gain an appreciation for the diversity and value of our own gifts as well as the diversity and gifts of others. This, in turn, will have an immediate and far-reaching effect upon each of the key elements of successful human systems: building healthier relationships, developing more effective communication, and gaining a greater understanding of ourselves and others.

We, the authors, are familiar with and continue to use many other models, tools, and approaches to personal and organizational development. But for us, nothing else compares with understanding the Jungian mental processes for simplicity, ease of access, and the depth and breadth of its power to change lives. When we begin to learn to recognize these processes, every relationship, every conversation, every introspective moment can become a lesson in appreciation for the amazing gifts that we all possess.

We invite you to join us on this journey. Whether your aim is to develop your own potential, improve your relationships, help others, bring your organization to the next level, or save the world, we know of no better place to start than right here.

ACKNOWLEDGMENTS

Over a decade ago, Leona Haas became concerned about the small but significant percent of people who have difficulty validating their reported type. These are the type users who do not feel that their type, as reported by the Myers-Briggs Type Indicator®, fits them very well. Faced with the challenges of sorting out their "true type" from their "reported type," many of these new users dismiss the instrument altogether and never come to benefit from its insights. It was this issue of type validation that gave the initial impetus to a journey that has taken Leona to an increasingly refined understanding of the Jungian mental processes and the dynamic system in which they operate. *Building Blocks of Personality Type* is the culmination of that journey.

There have been many teachers, guides, and helpers along the way, and it seems appropriate to acknowledge their contributions by relating a brief history.

Like many journeys, this one started at home. Leona was perplexed by the differences between the ways her husband, Rich, used his Sensing process and what she had learned about Sensing from her studies and from working extensively with type with federal government employees. When assembling a kit, for example, Rich never read directions. He preferred to work from pictures or by seeing the finished product. He also did not have good recall of past events and seemed to make intuitive leaps from what he observed. None of this fit with Sensing as Leona knew it.

In the early nineties very little information was readily available to the personality type community concerning Jung's views on the mental processes. *Gifts Differing* by Isabel Myers provided basic information about the eight Jungian processes, but many of Isabel's insights and most of her research had not been published.

Gradually, through her empirical work with type, Leona began to recognize that Sensing can be used in very different ways. When she started to divide her workshop participants into "SJ" and "SP" groups (thus distinguishing those with a preference for Introverted Sensing from those who prefer Extraverted Sensing), patterns began to emerge. She realized that her husband used Extraverted Sensing, while the military culture, in which she worked, tended to favor Introverted Sensing.

Having solved the mystery of Rich's Sensing preference by distinguishing Extraverted Sensing from Introverted, Leona began to suspect that she was learning about something which could enable type practitioners to help people more easily and clearly validate their type. The pursuit of a deeper understanding of the Myers-Briggs Type Indicator® became her passion.

First, she went back to the basics: to Carl Jung. She soon discovered the work of Daryl Sharp, a Toronto Jungian analyst and publisher of Jungian books. Sharp's book *Personality Types* was a gift of knowledge for her. In it, he explains the mental processes with unusual clarity. It opened a whole new level of understanding to Leona and helped to focus her investigations.

While attending courses through Type Resources, Leona met Gary and Margaret Hartzler and soon became a Qualifying Program instructor. Margaret and Gary were also doing research into the Jungian mental processes by investigating the theoretical concepts and incorporating them into their Qualifying Program. Leona's focus upon the practical aspects of the processes and the Hartzlers' work with the theory grew into a synergistic joint effort that allowed all three of them to develop and expand their understanding of the dynamics of type.

Over the course of the next five years, Leona developed ways of incorporating the Jungian processes into her feedback sessions. In 2000 she wrote *Journey of Understanding* with Margaret Hartzler and Bob McAlpine.

Katharine D. Myers is co-author of *Introduction to Type® Dynamics and Development*, the only book that Leona was able to find for her early research on type dynamics and development. Along with Daryl Sharp's work, it opened many doors of understanding for her. For the first time, she really began to understand individuation and how it related to personality type. During her research, she was very fortunate to have Kathy Myers become interested in her unique approach to exploring type feedback. Since then, Kathy's dedication and love for the MBTI® instrument and her steadfast guardianship of its ethical use has fanned the flame of Leona's enthusiasm and bolstered her courage to continue exploring this unfamiliar territory.

Her next major breakthrough came from the research and work of Dr. John Beebe, a Jungian analyst from San Francisco and past president of the San Francisco Jungian Institute. Dr. Beebe had been working on an enhanced theory of personality type, which is built upon the view that each psychological type encompasses eight distinct cognitive processes, rather than just four. His audiotape *A New Model of Psychological Types* revealed to Leona the tremendous scope of the insights contained within the type model. John has been a wonderful gift to the community of personality type practitioners. He is very supportive of the instrument and has done much to bring the Jungian and personality type communities closer together.

As early as 1974, Dr. Beebe developed the idea that the first four functions alternate attitudes like a series of checks and balances, with the third being in the same attitude as the first. He first presented this model at the 1983 Chiron Conference in New Mexico under the title "Psychological Types in Transference, Countertransference, and the Therapeutic Interaction." The following year that paper was published as a chapter in *Transference Countertransference*. By 1985, he had begun exploring the concept that each individual has access to all eight of the processes.

Each of the people mentioned above has, in his or her own way, been a pivotal source of the inspiration, information, and innovation that has shaped the eight-process model of type.

The collaboration to create this book began at a workshop that Leona led for the Vermont chapter of the Association for Psychological Type in January 2001. When Mark Hunziker asked how he could learn more, Leona recommended several books and tapes. She noted that while each explained a different element of her presentation, a comprehensive portrait of the model did not yet exist. She wanted to record a complete description, but her forte is live presentations, not writing. Encouraged and facilitated by Leona's friend Mary Thompson, the project was virtually launched after only an hour of conversation. Mark would have an opportunity to study the eight-process model up close, and with his help, Leona would be able to make her work available to a wider audience. Two Introverted Intuiting types do not need much information or time to know when something "fits"!

Like C. G. Jung and Isabel Myers, Leona has constantly tested, modified, and validated her theoretical understanding through literally thousands of conversations and observations. We are deeply indebted to the countless people with whom we have discussed type at workshops, training sessions, and elsewhere. These conversations have helped us to modify, clarify, and enhance our understanding of the theory as well. Most of the stories and statements that we use to draw portraits of the mental processes (chapters 4 through 11) are paraphrased combinations of comments from several people who share the preference, and a few are direct quotes. Though we cannot acknowledge everyone by name, we will be forever grateful for your contributions to our understanding. The only way that we can possibly begin to repay your willingness to share your stories and insights is by passing along what we have learned to others.

We are particularly grateful to those who have actively supported and aided our efforts to expand our understanding through their continued correspondence and friendship and, in some cases, their helpful feedback during the writing of this book.

Neither of us could have managed to pull this project together without the daily emotional and logistical support of our life partners, families, and friends. They have our profound appreciation and our love.

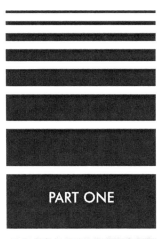

PART ONE

AN INTRODUCTION TO THE
EIGHT-PROCESS
MODEL OF TYPE

CHAPTER 1

TERMS AND CONCEPTS

Since a primary benefit of the eight-process model is that it provides a simple and direct route into the heart of personality type, we have taken pains in this book to present the underlying theory as simply as possible and to minimize the use of terms that are unfamiliar to the new learner. But some of the jargon is unavoidable, and a basic understanding of the theory behind the model is needed to provide context and perspective. You will find a glossary, along with several appendices, in the back of this book to help clarify and elaborate upon what we mention in the text, and to introduce some more advanced concepts that we cannot explore in depth here. This chapter provides a brief overview of the terms and concepts, along with a few miscellaneous tips.

It is not the purpose of typology to classify human beings into categories—this in itself would be pretty pointless. Its purpose is rather to provide a critical psychology which would make a methodical investigation and presentation . . . possible.

Carl G. Jung

THE MBTI® PERSONALITY INVENTORY

The Myers-Briggs Type Indicator® personality inventory is based on a model that was conceived by Swiss psychoanalyst Carl Gustav Jung and further developed by the team of Katharine Briggs and her daughter Isabel Briggs Myers. The MBTI® instrument is the most widely used, and the most rigorously validated, personality assessment tool in the world—with over three million people using it every year. Using a carefully crafted and statistically sound questionnaire, it is designed to identify an individual's mental process preference: how the person tends to gather information and make decisions. Many readers are familiar with the sixteen possible iterations of type that are represented by the indicator's well-known four-letter type code. The code identifies each individual's preferred ways of acquiring information and making decisions. By answering a series of standard questions, each person supplies the information needed by the indicator to arrive at a "reported type." However, since there are factors which may throw off these results, it is up to each individual to check the validity for themselves. By paying attention to how they actually tend to operate in their daily life, they will either confirm, or "verify," their reported preferences, or modify them to a better fitting "true type."

In verifying their type, new learners will need to notice not only how they gather information and make decisions, but also whether they tend to be more energized when they focus on their external environment or when they focus on their inner world, and whether their primary external focus is on making decisions or on taking in information. Thousands of trained professionals are qualified to administer the MBTI® instrument and help with verification, and are ready to provide feedback and support to help their clients understand type and apply that understanding to specific issues.

There is no way around the fact that a significant amount of information is needed in order to understand type at even the beginner level. But the sixteen personality profiles that have been the primary tool for introducing type can be unnecessarily intimidating to the new learner. Isabel Myers herself wrote that "the obvious obstacle" to gaining a comfortable familiarity with the types is that there are "too many to keep in mind by brute memory."[1] Using this approach, extensive professional support is often needed at the initial feedback/verification stage to bring people to a level of understanding where they are even able to see what it is that the model has to offer.

However, by approaching type first through the eight processes, its complexity is broken down into the most basic, most important, and least intimidating pieces: the mental processes themselves. These mental processes truly are the building blocks of personality. Only the most elementary understanding of the theory is needed initially, and feedback can focus on just the two most key and most easily verified elements, the dominant and auxiliary processes. If new learners are first grounded in the basic theory and armed with descriptions of the mental processes themselves, then they can truly understand the more complex type profile descriptions. The profiles do not need to be the starting point for teaching and feedback. Verification becomes easier because the learners have been given both the conceptual framework and the descriptions needed for sorting out why some aspects of their reported type profile may not seem to fit. They can see that every individual personality is a dynamic custom fit, woven from the processes.

On the other hand, those new learners who are first exposed to their reported type through a generic descriptive "profile" often misunderstand the intent of the profile. They may see it as an off-the-rack mass-produced item to be either accepted or rejected depending upon how well it seems to fit initially. Too often, when the profile does not fit perfectly, the credibility of the instrument itself is questioned. Too many people lose interest and do not stay with it long enough to reap the benefits of exploring type.

Learning about type primarily through the sixteen profiles can also lead to the misconception that these portraits tell us all that we need to know about personality. But most profiles are really just generalized descriptions of the traits and behaviors that reflect the dominant and auxiliary mental processes. If we are distracted by these descriptions and focus upon what we see on the surface without some understanding of the rich, complex, and dynamic psychic life from which it springs, we will overlook much of what the type model has to offer.

The type code itself is the starting place, designed primarily to facilitate easy access to our own type. None of the four dimensions of personality that are represented by the letters truly stands alone. Isabel said that "the traits that result from each preference do not combine to influence an individual's personality by simple addition of characteristics; instead, the traits result from the interaction of the preferences."[2] Each letter of the code represents an aspect of a very complex living system. When we look at these pieces together, in the natural system of the individual personality, we see that they interact in a myriad of fascinating and important ways. It is through understanding these *dynamics* of type that much of the model's insight into human personality can be found. The authors view the eight-process approach as an important guide for the complex task of seeking to understand this interaction of processes. It is an aid to help us raise our level of sophistication in order to grasp and use a much greater portion of the type model's underappreciated richness of insight and, from there, to continue to build and expand the scope of how we view and teach type.

We firmly believe that even those who have never been exposed to a personality type instrument can benefit from the information presented in this book. This approach of focusing on the individual processes is easy for anyone to absorb and use, and the potential for expanded understanding and for personal growth is enormous, even if this is a person's first encounter with the concept of mental processes.

For these new learners, the ideal learning approach is to use the material we are presenting in tandem with a skilled type professional. If you have the opportunity, we recommend that you take the MBTI® personality inventory, then use our book to boost your learning curve and augment the work you do with your consultant. If you use this approach, you will be amazed at how quickly your understanding will expand.

Most experienced type practitioners will find that they too can quickly reach a deeper level of appreciation of the dynamics of type through the eight-process model and that this perspective will almost automatically lead to more effective ways of working with clients. In chapter fourteen we outline some of the directions that these practical applications can take. You will also find exercises that will help facilitate interpretation and your clients' self-verification of their true type in *Journey of Understanding*[3] and *Functions of Type*.[4]

THE EIGHT-PROCESS MODEL

As we will show in the following pages, a basic working understanding of the mental processes does not absolutely require an interpreter. With just a little guidance, anyone can start this journey and reap significant benefits from the very beginning. By first simply focusing on the processes themselves, even the casual learner will benefit. On the other hand, those who choose to continue on this path by learning more about the theory upon which the model is based will have access to a depth of understanding that goes far beyond anything that most of us ever imagined.

In recent years, a few people, building upon the work of the pioneers of personality type, have developed some key refinements of how our mental processes are viewed. They have expanded our ability to understand these psychological mechanisms that we all use to cope, survive, and live our daily lives. Since the mental processes are such a big part of who we are and how we operate, any enhancement of our understanding of them is truly big news. This expanded view of type is what we are calling the "eight-process model."

An attitude of continuous exploration, expansion, and refinement of Jung's theory of personality types is very much in keeping with Jung's own perspective on his work. Marie-Louise von Franz, his close friend and professional collaborator, wrote: "He was a pioneer and remained fully aware that an enormous number of further questions remained un-answered and call for further investigation. This is why his concepts and hypotheses are conceived on as wide a basis as possible (without making them too vague and all-embracing) and why his views form a so-called 'open system' that does not close the door against new discoveries."[5]

Two crucial shifts in emphasis form the cornerstones of the eight-process approach to type. As noted earlier, neither is new. They actually just reemphasize what Jung and Myers had have been telling us all along. But refocusing on these key pieces of the foundation of type can have a far-reaching effect on how the model is understood and used.

THE FIRST CORNERSTONE

At any point in time, an individual is operating primarily from a single mental process (i.e., one function: Sensing, Intuiting, Thinking, or Feel-ing in either its Extraverted or Introverted attitude). That one process is the most crucial factor in understanding what is going on with that person at that moment. By shifting our focus from a complex profile of functions and attitudes to just the process that is being used at any given moment, we can actually grasp more of what is important with far more clarity and ease than if we try to look at all the possible factors at once. A majority of new learners find it much easier to verify or confirm their true type through this approach. They begin to understand why the profile for their reported type does not fit perfectly with what they know about themselves. When seen in terms of preferred mental processes, it becomes easier to see that the individual idiosyncrasies of normal per-sonality development are quite consistent with the generalizations of the type model. Thus, emphasizing the processes themselves avoids the negative experience of feeling put in a box—labeled and constricted by type—which some new learners experience.

This is where the simplicity and accessibility of the eight-process approach comes from. New learners find that they can understand and remember the relatively straightforward processes much more quickly and vividly than the profiles. They can watch clear examples in operation within themselves and others. Thus, through simple observation, they immediately begin to build an understanding of the different ways people operate. Process watching is the first step in learning about type through the eight-process approach.

THE SECOND CORNERSTONE

Everyone possesses the potential to use all eight of the mental processes. We each access and engage them in ways that are, to a great extent, universal and predictable, creating the sixteen innate and balanced sequences of processes that define the sixteen types. By learning about all eight of our process preferences, we can make predictions about how they may develop, how adroitly we will use them, how we will react to others who are using them, and the various ways in which they can manifest themselves throughout our lives.

Because it integrates the four processes that usually dwell in the unconscious along with the four that are more consciously accessible, the process-preference aspect of the approach can lead us into unlimited exploration and discovery of the complex and unique individuals that we are (see appendices B and E).

PROCESS WATCHING

The focus of this book is on the individual mental processes. Learning to recognize them is an enlightening experience unto itself, as well as the necessary first step for further exploration. No process description will fit you perfectly. Likewise, you may identify with some parts of all eight descriptions. You are a unique and complex being, and what we describe here is only, after all, a model that simplifies the description of personality and its development in order to help us to think and talk about it. This book focuses upon that model at its simplest level. In addition, it is important to realize that the model is a rational construct. It is a way to help us understand something that is inherently not rational and therefore can never be completely understood. Nevertheless, you will notice that some of the processes' descriptions resonate clearly within yourself, and you will begin to recognize some of them in the people around you as well. From this beginning, your recognition, understanding, and appreciation will continue to expand outward like ripples in a pond to encompass more and more of the actions and interactions around you.

We encourage you to read the descriptions; watch and listen for the processes in yourself and in others as you work and play, go back to the descriptions, then watch some more. It sounds too simple; however, the lessons to be learned from just process watching are virtually unlimited, and the potential for growth is truly profound.

MISCELLANEOUS TERMS

Throughout this book, when we talk about the eight processes, we are referring to what are often called the "Jungian mental processes." Those who are literate in the jargon of type will recognize our processes as the four functions of Sensing, Intuiting, Thinking, and Feeling in their Extraverted or Introverted attitudes. In other words, we are talking about the processes as they actually manifest themselves. We do not, for example, refer to Thinking as a process because there are actually two very different Thinking processes: Extraverted Thinking and Introverted Thinking.

We use the word "type" in reference to the understanding of sixteen personality types as represented by the four-letter type code. The type model theorizes that all human beings can be seen as using eight basic mental processes and that the inclination to prefer to use each process over others is innate in all of us. From these premises, the simple math of the type model creates sixteen possible sequences of process preferences: the sixteen types. Just as a four-letter type code is shorthand for a type, each type is actually shorthand for a constellation of process preferences. If we are able to grow and mature without unusual external pressures, we have the tendency to develop and use the eight processes in a natural pattern, according to this internal bias that we call "preference" (see appendices B and C). Our environment can influence our behavior and even our development but not our innate process preferences.

Some terms used in describing type have specialized definitions that differ from their common meanings. We often capitalize terms to warn you of their special use. For example, people who prefer a Judgment process are not necessarily more judgmental than others. Here, "Judgment" just means one of four ways to approach making a decision. Likewise, people using Thinking are not necessarily more intellectual, nor are those engaged in Feeling more sensitive, or those Extraverting more gregarious than anyone else. The irrational processes (the Perception processes: Extraverted and Introverted Sensing and Extraverted and Introverted Intuiting) are not necessarily unreasonable. They are called "irrational" because they are automatic. How we take in information (Perception) has nothing to do with reason (rational thought) one way or another.

Most type professionals still exclusively use the words coined by Jung about a century ago: Extraversion, Introversion, Sensation, and Intuition. We have found that many new learners find this a bit confusing. When we are talking about mental activity, it seems to work better to use active forms of the words. When people are interacting with the world around them, for example, we say that they are Extraverting. Likewise, when they are interacting with their personal, inner world, they are Introverting. We reserve the traditional terms for when we talk about the function or attitude itself. We use Jung's terms, for example, for the opposing sides of the perception dichotomy: Sensation and Intuition. On the other hand, when people are engaging these functions, we say that they are Sensing or Intuiting. We have found that new learners in particular relate better to these action words than to words that feel like labels.

As you read this book, if you find any terms mysterious or confusing, refer to the glossary for a concise definition and explanation.

LITERARY LICENSE

Jung's model does not explain everything about human psychology, but it is sometimes convenient for us to talk as if it does. Keep in mind that it is only a model, and for that matter, a model of mental processes only—not of traits, skills, or behavior. In chapters four through eleven, we do use extensive descriptions of traits and behavior as a way of helping you to recognize and understand the processes that tend to be associated with them. But what can be observed is actually just a reflection of the process, and that process, in turn, is only a representation of an important facet of how we humans operate. The model, wonderfully illuminating as it is, is just a way to help us think in simple terms about an incredibly complex phenomenon.

We admit to indulging in a bit of semi fiction in the way we describe the processes in this book: as if they exist in pure, well-developed, conscious, and mostly constructive forms. In the real world, the way that we engage the processes may be influenced by the situation, by developmental factors, by their position in the sequence of preference, or by another mental process. Even the people whose stories are reported in this book will not identify with all the stories or statements about their preferred process. This is because when we talk about a single mental process, we are taking it out of the context of the individual personality. The processes are never really separate or distinct from the unique living and dynamic system in which they operate. In action, they are never seen in isolation from other influences. But by oversimplifying our descriptions in this way, the processes become much more easily recognizable. Even though the "pure" process may exist only in theory, by talking in these terms we are describing the common elements that are in play whenever a given process is being used. Thus the process becomes easier to spot, regardless of how other influences may color and modify it.

We have also taken the convenient liberty of talking about the processes as if they are conscious beings with wills of their own. We say they "do" this and "want" that, as if they are individual characters in a play. This, of course, is not literally true at all. But it is a very handy and essentially accurate way to describe how they operate.

CHAPTER 2

TYPE THEORY IN BRIEF

WHAT IS PROCESS PREFERENCE?

In theory, each one of us has the ability to use all eight of the mental processes. We differ, typologically, by which ones we naturally prefer to use. Some processes are very comfortable and require little effort for us to bring them into play. They are a big part of who we are. They are like our favorite, most personal room in our home, the room that reflects who we are and is our safe haven where we can be ourselves. Our preference for these processes may be so clear and our ability to access them so well developed that we use them automatically, even when they may not be well suited to the situation at hand. This is simply human nature, like the preference for using our left or right hand.

At the other end of the preference spectrum are processes that are also a part of us but lie in our unconscious. Our awareness of them is usually marginal at best, and when we do engage them, it is likely to be an awkward and uncomfortable experience. We usually choose to simply avoid using them and perhaps even to deny their very existence. But, like wearing a path to a remote location, the more we use these unfamiliar processes and become accustomed to them, the easier it becomes. In fact, maturing to become a more balanced individual and growing toward our full potential is mostly a matter of becoming more and more adept at accessing those innately unconscious mental processes. Until we develop our awareness and appreciation for these processes, we miss out on their benefits. Even worse, they may be a frequent source of conflict or may bubble to the surface in times of stress, resulting in behavior that is inept, inappropriate, and seemingly out of character.

Experience shows that it is practically impossible, owing to adverse circumstances in general, for anyone to develop all his psychological functions simultaneously. The demands of society compel a man to apply himself first and foremost to the differentiation of the function with which he is best equipped by nature, or which will secure him the greatest social success. Very frequently, indeed as a general rule, a man identifies more or less completely with the most favored and hence the most developed function. It is this that gives rise to the various psychological types.

Carl G. Jung

OUR TWO MOST PREFERRED PROCESSES

In order to survive, every human being must have a way of acquiring information and a way of making decisions. The more adept we are at performing and balancing these two basic mental tasks, the more successful we are likely to be. As Isabel Myers put it: "The two skilled processes can develop side by side because they are not antagonistic . . . . Although one can assist the other, there should be no doubt which comes first. The stability of one process, unchallenged by the others, is essential to the stability of the individual. Each process has its own set of aims, and for successful adaptation, as Jung pointed out, the aims must be 'constantly clear and unambiguous.' One process needs to govern which way a person moves; it should always be the same process, so that today's move will not be regretted and reversed tomorrow."[6]

Convincing evidence indicates that it is more effective in the day-to-day business of coping and surviving to be an expert at using one approach for each of these tasks rather than to develop modest comfort with several. Adept use of any single approach to gathering data, teamed with a single well-developed way of making decisions, enables us to negotiate most of life's situations, even if we are not operating in ways that are ideally suited to the specific situation. When it comes to effectively engaging one of these coping strategies, process expertise is usually more crucial than process suitability.

Most of our psychic focus for the first two decades of our lives is normally upon developing extensive facility with just one mental process for each of the two basic tasks: gathering information and making decisions (see appendix C). The two processes that we prefer for these tasks are the ones that we tend to use the most and with which we feel most comfortable. They are the processes that will probably remain most closely associated with our personal identity for the rest of our lives. They are the processes that will resonate and have you saying "That's me!" as you read their descriptions in chapters four through eleven.

Since these processes complement each other, they are able to develop largely in tandem throughout the early years of our lives. But, as in a play, there can be only one lead role. It is this "dominant" process that usually reaches maturity first and is the most trusted of all. We rely on it consistently and regard it as the hero/heroine of our lifelong drama.[7]

This first process is the one that we can consciously call into play with the most ease and with the least expenditure of energy. It is the charismatic element of our personality. It is so important in how we operate mentally that it would not be an exaggeration to view the roles of all our other cast members as supporting this process, the star of the show.

The second of our dynamic duo of processes is the "auxiliary." It normally develops next and complements the dominant process in crucial ways. Between the two, one takes in information and the other makes decisions; one focuses on the environment and the other focuses within; one is rational and the other is irrational. In this way, the auxiliary supplies much of the balance that we need as we move through life.

The auxiliary process acts like a trusted adviser and a supportive parent to the dominant one. Because of its complementary nature, the second process is able to modify and balance the energy and enthusiasms of the first, thus lending a degree of maturity to the personality. Though never in the true leading role of our personal drama, the auxiliary process can sometimes be so influential and visible that it is mistaken for the star.

Together, these two characters are often capable of carrying off life's scenes with very little help from the other six cast members; and because they are usually so comfortable and so clearly preferred, they are frequently expected to do so. If your close friends were asked to describe your personality, the descriptions would be, for the most part, descriptions of these two primary processes in action. Personality type instruments are, in fact, a sophisticated way of identifying our two most preferred processes. Most type-related profiles that we see today primarily reflect the influences of the dominant and auxiliary processes.

Though identification of these two favored processes is critical, it is just the first step in solving our process-preference puzzle.

A SEQUENCE OF PREFERENCES

Building from the identification of our two most preferred processes—done usually through a personality type instrument—the eight-process model tells us how the other mental processes are aligned in an arrangement that includes all eight. This sequence tells us that with normal development, the processes line up from most preferred to least, from the one that is most conscious to the one that is most unconscious, from most adept and comfortable to the least, and from the one requiring the least energy to use to the one requiring the most. If we think of the processes as the actors in our personal drama, then it is their positions in the sequence that outline the roles they will play. *How* they will play those roles is determined by the personalities of the actors—by the nature of the processes themselves.

Of course, "normal" is just a mathematical concept. There are not actually any normal people, and none of us develops exactly according to the template of type or any other theory. But the type model has held up for over sixty years because of its usefulness in describing a typical sequence of psychological growth and because it provides a formula for maturity and balance that appears to be innate in all of us. The rich journey of self-discovery, for which type can act as our guidebook, is partly about understanding the universal aspects of type: how the characters in the cast of eight usually act and interact by virtue of their innate nature and assigned roles. It is also about how our own unique mix of developmental and situational factors modifies this interplay. As Jung put it, "conformity is one side of a man, uniqueness is the other."[8]

THE IMPORTANCE OF UNDERSTANDING OUR PREFERENCES

Within each constellation of eight processes lies an inexhaustible source of insight that is most easily and effectively accessed by patiently sifting down through its many layers, one at a time. Though this book focuses upon the simplest level, it is important to be aware that this journey can take us into the increasingly unfamiliar and uncomfortable territory of our less preferred and often unconscious mental processes.

The path to self-knowledge and self-management is best traveled one step at a time. It is not so intimidating this way, and with this approach, no matter how far you choose to go, you will be able to understand and integrate what you have experienced along the way. Since this introductory book focuses on recognition of the processes that we experience and see, we will look primarily at the dominant and (to a lesser extent) the auxiliary processes. These are the two processes that most people use and show most of the time. These are the processes that are visible in their purest forms, so process watching is initially about observing these most preferred processes.

"Being consciously aware of the way I tend to function makes it possible for me to assess my attitudes and behavior in a given situation and adjust them accordingly. It enables me both to compensate for my personal disposition and to be tolerant of someone who does not function as I do —someone who has, perhaps, a strength or facility I myself lack."[9]

Understanding how our own mental processes work is a tremendous gift unto itself, and the increased appreciation and valuing of other peoples' unique talents is another. An equally important benefit is that this understanding can help facilitate our own psychic and spiritual growth as human beings. As we go through our lives, we are driven to become whole, to be all that we can be. Even if personal growth is not our goal, it happens anyway when we explore our less developed mental processes. We gradually become more comfortable with the processes and are able to bring them to bear more effectively upon life's situations and issues. At the same time, we are becoming more comfortable with this strange mental territory —less afraid of what is deep inside ourselves and less annoyed or fearful when we see these processes manifested in others. Consequently, our unconscious processes become less likely to surface in unpredictable, immature, and counterproductive ways. This business of type development can enhance our personal capacities as well as our tolerance and appreciation of others, as we learn to accept and use more of the wide range of perception and decision-making approaches that are available within us all.

CHAPTER 3

FROM FOUR DICHOTOMIES TO EIGHT MENTAL PROCESSES TO SIXTEEN TYPES

WHY EIGHT PROCESSES?

Carl Jung described three distinct dimensions, or "dichotomies," of personality.[10] Each dichotomy is made up of two contrasting halves. Jung drew a line between the two sides of each dichotomy in much the same way that you might cut a cake in half. Using Jung's three dichotomies, we draw three sets of lines. We divide our cake first into halves, then into quarters, and finally into eight equal pieces.

First, we focus on the three dichotomies that were identified by Jung and adapted for the type code by Isabel Myers. These first three dichotomies are the ones that actually define the eight aspects of personality type.

"Orientation to the environment" is the dichotomy which Myers identified from allusions which Jung had made but had never formalized into a dichotomy. After we have identified the eight pieces, we will use this fourth dichotomy to guide us in arranging the eight mental processes to distinguish the sixteen types.

These four function types correspond to the obvious means by which consciousness obtains its orientation to experience. Sensation (i.e., sense perception) tells you that something exists; thinking tells you what it is; feeling tells you whether it is agreeable or not; and intuition tells you whence it comes and where it is going.
Carl G. Jung and M.-L. von Franz

The four-letter personality type code is divided into four dichotomies		
The dichotomies are about		
either . . .		. . . or
Extraverting	ENERGY	Introverting
Sensing	PERCEPTION	Intuiting
Thinking	JUDGMENT	Feeling
Judging	ENVIRONMENT	Perceiving

Now, let's walk through the steps that lead us from the first three dichotomies to eight mental processes.

We start with a whole circle, representing the entire personality. First, we divide our personality model into halves by distinguishing between the two basic purposes of mental processes: gathering information (Perception) and making decisions (Judgment).

Perception   **Judgment**

Next, our two pieces are divided again to become four. Perception is separated into the distinct approaches of Sensing Perception and Intuiting Perception. Judgment becomes Thinking Judgment and Feeling Judgment.

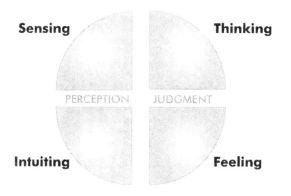

Sensing   **Thinking**

PERCEPTION   JUDGMENT

Intuiting   **Feeling**

We will return to our cake cutting shortly. First, let's look more closely at the four pieces that we have so far.

PERCEPTION AND JUDGMENT

As we have said, all human psychic activity can be viewed as being devoted to two simple tasks that are essential to our survival: taking in information and making decisions. Not much is going on that cannot be included in one of these basic process categories: we gather data, then we make choices. There are two dramatically different ways to approach each of these tasks.

Sensing Perception and Intuiting Perception

How we perceive or gather information provides the second letter of the type code. This letter will be either an S for Sensing or an N for Intuiting, as in ESTJ or ENTJ.

Perception is considered to be irrational because no intentional editing process is involved in selecting the information that is taken in. No one can take in all the data around us; there is just far too much of it. The two approaches to perception are essentially mechanisms that automatically restrict the flow of information by means of two very different focuses of attention. The same data is available to everyone with fully functional sensory organs, but what we actually perceive is what makes it through these innate filters to our awareness. Sensing and Intuiting simply notice different kinds of information.

Sensing (S)

The focus of Sensing is on information gathered by the five senses: what we see, hear, touch, smell, and taste. It can include memories of past sensations as well as sensations being experienced in the present. Sensing perceptions are always tangible and verifiable, at least in theory, even though they are not necessarily always clear or accurate.

Adept use of a Sensing process will balance, and thus soften, the tendency of a preferred Judging process to overlook concrete information in its rush to a decision.

Whether noticing their current environment or recalling past surroundings, people using a Sensing process tend to do so in vivid detail. They prefer to live in the real world of tangible things, past or present. They want to know who, what, where, and when.

Intuiting (N)

The focus of perception through Intuiting is on an expanded picture. Intuition may draw its information from the environment or from within. It attempts to extrapolate from seemingly random bits of information to understand the patterns or meanings that the data represents and thus to generate connections, meanings, possibilities, options, and vision. One cannot foresee or control the Intuiting processes' timetables, or methodologies.

The Intuiting mental processes work with content that varies widely from individual to individual and from moment to moment. A Sensing process, when observing a tree, for example, is always tied to data from the senses: shades of color, shapes, sizes, comparisons, and so on. An Intuiting process, on the other hand, may notice almost no concrete information before rapidly moving on to build a series of connections. It may generate possibilities or attach meaning and significance to the tree or create a broader mental picture of the forest. This picture may have no discernable relationship to anything that can be detected by the senses. The Intuitive search is for connections, patterns, and underlying significance.

Thinking Judgment and Feeling Judgment

How we judge or make decisions provides the third letter of the type code. This letter will be either a T for Thinking or an F for Feeling, as in INTJ or ENFJ.

The Judgment processes provide rational structure to our perceptions so that we can make use of the information gathered. They shape the actions of our conscious will. Since the task of a Judgment process is to make decisions, it is not surprising that both the Thinking and Feeling approaches are oriented toward reaching some kind of outcome.

Another way to describe what Judgment processes do is that they attempt to gain some internal or external control over our lives and our world. The need to influence events and situations and to act with purpose is an obvious requirement for survival, and it is what decision making through Thinking or Feeling is all about.

Thinking (T)

The Thinking approach to decision making is essentially that of analytical logic. To support this analysis, it uses criteria that it either pulls from the environment or synthesizes internally in order to define everything. Though it may sometimes seem to others as if these judgments devalue people and things by pigeonholing them, they actually have nothing to do with value at all. Thinking processes simply need to attach a label or category to everything in order to understand its position relative to the rest of the universe, to maintain a sense of order, and to fit it into some kind of logical framework for the analysis that leads to decisions.

Thinking is impersonal. It intentionally excludes values-based considerations. Most people with a Thinking preference would rather be truthful than tactful and are more interested in being fair than in being kind.

Feeling (F)

Feeling is a values-based approach to Judgment. It determines what something is worth. Feeling is aware of the impact of its choices. It is aware of the individuals involved and affected, their circumstances, and their relationships. Creating and maintaining external or internal harmony is, therefore, the primary priority of the decision making. In the personality type model, the term "Feeling" simply refers to decision-making processes that are guided by systems of values. A preference for Feeling does not have anything to do with emotions. Feeling types are neither more nor less inclined to be emotional than Thinking types.

While no less rational than Thinking, Feeling is certainly not constrained by logic, often caring more about tact than truth and about the effect of a decision than about being right.

Now let's return to our cake. We have already used two of the dichotomies to arrive at the four "pieces" that we have described. Finally, each of these four is divided again, according to whether they are Extraverted or Introverted. As shown below, we now have eight equal pieces: the eight mental processes of type.

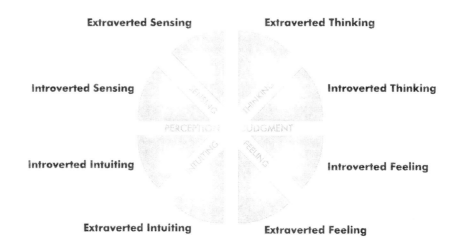

Extraverted Sensing

Extraverted Thinking

Introverted Sensing

Introverted Thinking

Introverted Intuiting

Introverted Feeling

Extraverted Intuiting

Extraverted Feeling

EXTRAVERTING AND INTROVERTING

The energy preference provides the first letter of the type code. This letter will be either an E for Extraverting or an I for Introverting, as in *ESTP* or *ISTP*.

The final division of the psychic cake, the one that brings us to the eight distinct mental processes, is the difference between Extraverting and Introverting the four functions of Sensing, Intuiting, Thinking, and Feeling. Each one of the four can have either the external world or the internal world as its focus. As Jung put it, "there are no Extraverts or Introverts pure and simple; only extraverted and introverted function types."[11] It is this Extraverting or Introverting orientation that distinguishes whether the focus of that process is the objective world around us or the subjective world within. It is referred to as the energy dichotomy because it reflects how we focus our personal energy: externally or internally.

Though last in our presentation of the factors that delineate the eight processes, the Extraverting/Introverting aspect is certainly not the least impactful. It is, in fact, the one that Jung noticed first and is a distinction of utmost importance.

Extraverting (E)

If our most skilled, trusted, and comfortable process—our dominant process—is Extraverted, we usually put our best face forward. By definition, we must all "extravert" in order to interact with people and the rest of the physical world. So the processes that we directly and most easily observe in people are usually their Extraverted processes. Because of this, it has become a common misconception that only the Extraverted processes can be observed by others.

In people who prefer Extraverting, what we most readily observe usually reflects their most comfortable process. Thus, individuals who prefer Extraverting are typically accessible and relatively easy for others to understand. What you see is what you get. Sharing experiences with others is, after all, an essential ingredient of Extraverting. People whose dominant process is Extraverted feature their most talented actor at center stage in the starring role.

By virtue of their objective focus upon their environment and their extensive interaction with it, people who prefer Extraverting tend to be aware of and in tune with a broad scope of external information.

As Sharp noted, "When one is predominantly oriented to the object—things and other people—there is an extraverted type."[12] If a process focuses on the environment, we call it Extraverted because it draws its energy from interacting with the external object, person, or situation, much as we are warmed and energized by the sun. An individual who prefers Extraverting is fueled by the situation itself.

Introverting (I)

Introverted processes focus on a subjective inner psychic life of reflection, concepts, and ideas. The outer world of tangible things and people may be integrated into this inner world, but the real excitement and energy of Introverting come from these personal thoughts and ideas. In fact, when Introverting we may not need external input at all, working entirely within ourselves. Sharp says that "While the extravert responds to what comes to the subject from the object (outer reality), the introvert relates mainly to the impressions aroused by the object in the subject (inner reality)."[13]

People whose most preferred process is Introverted do not usually show the world their greatest gifts. When they speak or take action in the world, they usually do so through their auxiliary process, so observers can never observe the dominant process directly. The Extraverted auxiliary process is the one featured in the spotlight and is often mistakenly assumed to be the star.

The focus of the auxiliary process is always complementary to the dominant. Because of this, observers often see and hear one thing, while the person who prefers Introverting is actually coming from a very different place. For example, we may hear what sounds like a decision. But if the speaker has an Introverted dominant preference for Perceiving, that person may actually be just trying to share information that he or she has acquired. These perceptions, however, are filtered and reframed as they are expressed (Extraverted) through their auxiliary Judging process and emerge into the world sounding like a decision.

This is not to say that Introverted processes cannot be observed. They can. In observing any process, even an Extraverted one, we are, of course, actually observing the outward manifestations of a mental activity. For Introverted processes, these visible clues are usually just more subtle and require closer attention to detect than their externally-oriented counterparts. They do not proceed aloud or publicly. But you can see people withdraw as they engage their Introverted processes. They may have a distant, unfocused look in their eyes or look down or away from others. When they refocus, you may have further evidence that they have been Introverting in the personal, subjective, and original nature of the information or decisions they report.

With those who prefer Introverting, what you see is usually not their dominant, preferred process. Introverting, by its very nature, cannot be shared directly. An Introverted process draws energy from what is going on inside, as when we are warmed from within by metabolizing our food. An individual who prefers Introverting is fueled by contemplation.

ORIENTATION TO THE ENVIRONMENT: KEY TO THE TYPE CODE

The fourth and final letter of the type code indicates what an individual prefers to do in the external world: either make decisions or gather information. This letter will be either a J for Judging or a P for Perceiving, as in ENT*J* or ENT*P*.

We can see that the first three dichotomies of type, represented in the first three letters of the type code, define all eight of the mental processes: Extraverted Sensing, Introverted Sensing, Extraverted Intuiting, Introverted Intuiting, Extraverted Thinking, Introverted Thinking, Extraverted Feeling, and Introverted Feeling. The fourth dichotomy, or the fourth letter, is needed primarily to show the order of an individual's natural preferences for engaging those processes. By telling us whether a person's preferred "orientation to the environment" is for Judging or Perceiving, the entire sequence of preference for using the eight processes is revealed.

The addition of the final dichotomy was Isabel Myers's great gift to the world. It tells us through which function—either the decision-making (Judgment) or the data-gathering (Perception) function—we prefer to interact with our external environment. This is the piece of information that assembled Jung's theories of personality into a complete system. It is what makes it possible to summarize rich and complex theory in a simple formula that even new learners can grasp.

To recap: the four letters of the type code represent the four dichotomies of personality type.		
First Letter	E (Extraverting) or I (Introverting)	Energy
Second Letter	S (Sensing) or N (Intuiting)	Perception
Third Letter	T (Thinking) or F (Feeling)	Judgment
Fourth Letter	J (Judging) or P (Perceiving)	Environment Orientation

HOW TYPE CODE INTERPRETATION WORKS

The first three dichotomies, each with its two opposing halves, create eight possible mental processes. Now we will take you through the steps used in interpreting the code. These are the steps that connect any four-letter code reported by a personality type instrument to the sequence of mental processes that describes that type. The steps will be similar to those in our cake-cutting exercise but in a different order. If you find the mechanics of interpretation confusing, do not worry. You are not alone, and you do not need to understand the details in order to understand type. Qualified type professionals receive extensive training in order to interpret the personality type code.

Understanding at least the general idea of type interpretation is important because it is central to understanding the model. The framework of personality type contains a limitless depth of insight into personality. But Isabel Myers had to form the model into a deceptively simple code because her central purpose in creating the instrument was to provide everyone access, through interpretation, to an understanding of his or her own type.

Interpretation is where the fourth dichotomy comes into play. When we interpret a type code, this last dichotomy is actually our starting point. A four-step process is used to find the dominant and auxiliary processes for each of the four-letter type codes.

In order to facilitate our understanding of the four-letter type code we need to distinguish between the attitudes and the functions. Based on the work of Carl Jung, Extraverting and Introverting are called "attitudes." Isabel Myers added Judging and Perceiving as attitudes. The middle letters of the type code are called "functions." Thus, Sensing, Intuiting, Thinking, and Feeling are all functions.

STEP 1: DETERMINE WHICH OF THE TWO PREFERRED FUNCTIONS IS EXTRAVERTED

In the first step of interpretation, the J or P of Myers's environmental dichotomy provides the key to determining the Extraverted function.[14] For the ESFJ type, for example, the J indicates that the Judging function (which the third letter of the formula shows is F for Feeling) is the preferred way of interacting with the environment. In other words, we know that one of ESFJ's two most preferred processes is Extraverted Feeling.

Applying the same logic to the ISFP type, the P indicates that the Perceiving function (which the second letter of the code shows is S for Sensing) is the preferred means of interacting with the environment. For ISFP, Sensing is Extraverted.

FIRST EXAMPLE

In ESFJ: The Judging (J) function is Feeling (F), so the Extraverted process would be Extraverted Feeling (Fe).

SECOND EXAMPLE

In ISFP: The Perceiving (P) function is Sensing (S), so the Extraverted process would be Extraverted Sensing (Se).

Step 1:
What is Extraverted?

The fourth letter indicates whether it is the Judgment function (a T or an F) or the Perception function (an S or an N) that is Extraverted.

STEP 2: DETERMINE WHICH OF THE TWO FUNCTIONS IS INTROVERTED

In step 2, we use the principle of balance and the logic of simple elimination to deduce that the other function in the four-letter code (S, N, T, or F) is Introverted. For ESFJ, since Feeling was Extraverted, then the remaining function, Sensing, must be Introverted.

For ISFP, since Sensing was Extraverted, then the remaining function, Feeling, must be Introverted.

In ESFJ: Sensing (S) is Introverted (Si).

In ISFP: Feeling (F) is Introverted (Fi).

Step 2:
What is Introverted?

Our functions are identified by the two middle letters of the code. If, in Step 1, we found that we Extravert the function identified by the second letter, then we know that we Introvert the function identified by the third letter. If we found that we Extravert the third letter, then we must Introvert the second letter.

STEP 3: DETERMINE WHICH OF THE TWO PREFERRED FUNCTIONS IS THE DOMINANT PROCESS

Step 3 focuses on the first letter of the type code to identify the most preferred, or dominant, mental process. Steps 1 and 2 identify the most

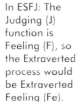

preferred Extraverted function and the most preferred Introverted function. The first letter of the code indicates which one of these is our dominant process. Note that in the type code or when they stand alone, the letters E and I are traditionally capitalized. When they are combined with a letter representing a function (such as T for Thinking) to indicate a mental process (such as Introverted Thinking), they are lowercase (Ti).

In our first example, ESFJ, the E indicates that the Extraverted function (which has already been determined to be Feeling) is the most preferred. Thus, for ESFJ, Extraverted Feeling is the dominant process.

In the second example, the I shows that Introverted Feeling is the dominant mental process for ISFP.

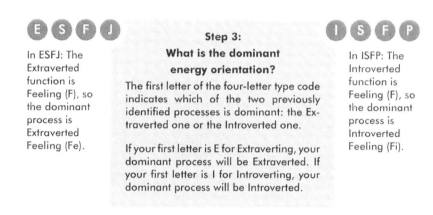

In ESFJ: The Extraverted function is Feeling (F), so the dominant process is Extraverted Feeling (Fe).

Step 3:
What is the dominant energy orientation?

The first letter of the four-letter type code indicates which of the two previously identified processes is dominant: the Extraverted one or the Introverted one.

If your first letter is E for Extraverting, your dominant process will be Extraverted. If your first letter is I for Introverting, your dominant process will be Introverted.

In ISFP: The Introverted function is Feeling (F), so the dominant process is Introverted Feeling (Fi).

STEP 4: DETERMINE WHICH OF THE TWO PROCESSES IS THE AUXILIARY PROCESS

Step 4 identifies our second-most preferred, or auxiliary, process. This is simply the process we identified earlier that is not the dominant one. For ESFJ, Introverted Sensing is the auxiliary process. For ISFP, Extraverted Sensing is the auxiliary process.

Step 4 is a great illustration of how Myers created a practical application from Jung's theory. Jung observed that the psyche has a need to balance the purpose and orientation of the dominant process. In the first example, the dominant Judging function needs to be balanced by a Perceiving function in the "trusted adviser" role and the dominant orientation to Extraverting balanced by Introverting. Similarly, in the second example, the dominant Introverted Judging function needs the balance of an Extraverted Perceiving function.

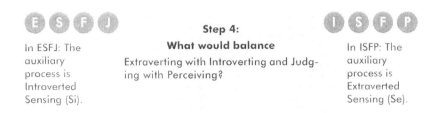

Step 4:

What would balance

Extraverting with Introverting and Judging with Perceiving?

In ESFJ: The auxiliary process is Introverted Sensing (Si).

In ISFP: The auxiliary process is Extraverted Sensing (Se).

As we have shown, the interpretation of the type code identifies not only what our two preferred processes are but also which one we prefer most (our dominant) and which is second (our auxiliary). The need for balance applies to all eight of the mental processes, creating sixteen possible type sequences in which the processes are arranged by preference. Thus, we have a total of sixteen possible personality types.

Eight very different type codes contain a J as the last letter.

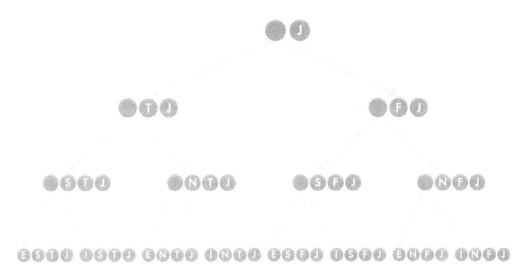

The other eight very different type codes contain a P as the last letter.

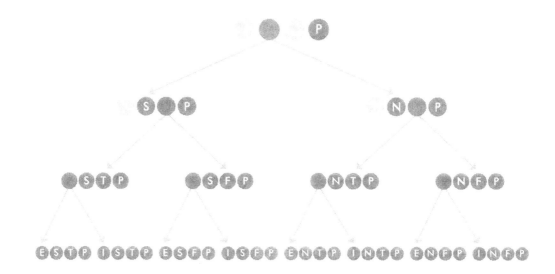

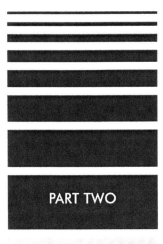

PART TWO

THE EIGHT
JUNGIAN
MENTAL PROCESSES

CHAPTER 4

EXTRAVERTED SENSING (Se)

In this chapter, we seek to present a picture of the "pure" Extraverted Sensing that we would see if we could carefully remove it from its natural state where it is influenced and colored by all the other elements of personality. Though no process actually exists separated from the rest of the personality, the portrait that follows reflects core characteristics that are in play whenever Extraverted Sensing is engaged at a conscious level.

Extraverted Sensing most clearly resembles the descriptions in the following pages when it is in the dominant (first) position. In fact, these descriptions are based on input from people for whom the process is dominant (ESTP and ESFP). But even with Extraverted Sensing in the first position, what you observe will vary noticeably depending on other factors—particularly whether it is paired up with Introverted Thinking or Introverted Feeling in the auxiliary (second) position.

In order to draw a complete picture of the "essence" of Extraverted Sensing, one must use bits and pieces that cannot individually demonstrate "pure" Se. Like the splashes of color in an impressionist painting, however, the bullets in this chapter, when taken all together, reveal a vivid portrait that will enable you to recognize Extraverted Sensing when you see it. Knowing what the process would look like if it could be separated from other influences is the foundation of process watching, the practice that will quickly take you as far as you want to go in understanding personality.

Extraverted Sensing is an information-gathering process. It focuses on the current objective, external world to fully experience the details of the environment through the five senses. Se draws energy and enjoyment directly from people, objects, and events.

**Dominant for
ESTP and ESFP**

**Auxiliary for
ISTP and ISFP**

KEY FEATURES

Extraverted Sensing

- Has an outer focus on acquiring information through the five senses.
- Is the only perception process that is not influenced by associations from the past, present, or future.
- Is aware of and connected to the current external environment.
- Quickly notices objective facts with all the details.
- Relies heavily on unusually accurate visual perception: seeing is believing.
- Values the object itself, not one's personal reaction or relationship to it.
- Seeks the full sensory experience of the environment in the moment.

WHAT'S GOING ON?

Extraverted Sensing

- Looks at things objectively and sees what is physically there.
- Gathers pure, unfiltered sensory information from the external world.
- Takes in the current environment as a collection of discrete bits of detailed information.
- Constantly seeks variety and novelty as sensory experiences change from moment to moment.
- Needs the immediate sensation of an external object, person, or event in order to have an experience. There is no experience without active involvement in the environment through one or more of the senses.
- Appreciates vivid details: colors, sounds, smells, tastes, and textures.
- Seeks raw, unsorted, unaltered experiences in order to feel alive.
- Is energized by the current experience.

When people are using their preferred Extraverted Sensing

- Their awareness is entirely focused upon the here and now.
- Virtually everything that can be detected by the senses gets noticed.
- The trigger for perception is the current external environment.
- The world consists only of what can be perceived by the five senses right now.
- Detailed visual perception is particularly important.

A level of attention is sustained that would quickly put others on "data overload."

They do not want to miss anything.

They value practical, hands-on experiences above all.

Memories from the past and possibilities for the future are not very important.

They are acutely aware of what is.

Their perceptions are verifiable.

Everything is a new experience. No two moments or situations are exactly the same.

Anything that is tangible is interesting.

Immediate sensory experience is what life is all about. It defines one's existence.

Life is one continual sensual experience.

They are enjoying life to the fullest, living for today.

The current experience itself has intensity.

FROM THE OUTSIDE, LOOKING IN

When we experience people who are engaging their preferred Extraverted Sensing, they

Seem to need almost constant external stimulation or they quickly become bored.

Seem to miss nothing and overlook no detail of the immediate environment.

Can be prone to repeating mistakes by failing to anticipate what is going to happen in the future as a consequence of what is happening now.

Can be reflective, but the reflections are tied to the current world.

Often have difficulty doing the steps of an operation in an orderly sequence. They prefer a random, "take it as it comes" approach.

Possess practical, hands-on skills.

Are very down-to-earth, realistic, and pragmatic.

Speak about objective facts: what is there, no more and no less.

Talk in very literal terms using concrete, sensory, and descriptive present-tense language: "I smell, I hear, I see."

Often show attention by focusing their eyes or tilting their ears or head toward you.

- Sometimes can be seen darting their eyes all around the room, observing everything.
- Listen at first to people telling of their experiences but do not have a need for, or a high interest in, hearing someone else's stories.
- Want information from others but not in too much detail. They cannot experience the world through other people's interpretations.
- Often listen with intense, focused attention. Their eyes lock on you, following your every gesture. They may move closer or lean in. They are so focused on taking in information that they may show no reaction to what you are saying.
- Pick up on other people's body language and other signals and will often automatically mirror them.
- Tend to use and need nonverbal communication, such as a smile, a wink, or a touch.
- Appear to accept life as it happens.
- Seem to relate easily to people, to enjoy being with people.
- Appear to accept people for who they are—to have few illusions about them.
- Can be perceived as shallow because of their outward tendency to "go with the flow."
- Are always interacting with the environment.
- Tend to be quick to assess data and to size up a situation.
- Do not seem to feel a need to conform to what others think is acceptable, assuming that people simply have their own unique styles.
- Are usually active, restless, and adventurous.
- Sometimes seem like hyperactive children. The immediate environment is constantly stimulating and distracting them.
- Are engaging, fun-loving, and social.
- Are very spontaneous and react quickly to changes in their environment.
- Can blend into almost any culture, environment, or situation.

CONTRIBUTIONS

Special perspectives and approaches of Extraverted Sensing

- A "live for today" attitude
- Learn quickly from experience
- An aptitude for learning new languages, including the subtle details of intonation and gestures
- Negotiate by quickly getting to the core of the matter
- Reliability in observing and reporting objective facts
- A knack for being a "mover and shaker" when it comes to concrete tasks
- Can quickly find practical solutions, to find an immediate fix for a problem
- A willingness to help, to play the role of a good Samaritan

FROM THE INSIDE

Paraphrased descriptions of what it is like to gather information through one's preferred Extraverted Sensing

- I need to actually experience something in order to understand it. I need to either look at a bicycle or at a picture of a bike in order to assemble one. Then I can duplicate what I see. Written instructions are not very helpful.
- I personally hate history. I figure if it's already happened, then who cares?
- I need to see and experience something before I believe it. I'm the classic "doubting Thomas."
- In a restaurant, I can be completely attentive to the conversation and interaction at our table and also know everything that's going on in other parts of the room.
- I let life happen rather than trying to control it.
- As a child I had to touch everything. I still do. The textures and colors just grab me.
- I love to be outside, feeling the sun and the breeze, hearing the insects and the birds. I love the feel of soil on my hands, planting flowers, and pulling weeds.
- The first thing in the morning, I look outside to check the weather. Then I turn on the news to see what's happening in the rest of the world.

- I never watch a taped game or event. If it has already happened, what is the sense of watching?
- Other adults seem to constantly be telling kids "Don't touch!" "Don't put that in your mouth!" But I can relate to the young child's fascination with exploring and experiencing the environment.
- I don't do lists, not even grocery lists. What I buy is what catches my eye. I walk up and down the aisles looking for items that look interesting.
- I can be observant at the expense of imagination.
- If you want to get my attention, tell me a story with concrete images.
- Give me the information I need to do the job, and then let me do it.
- I show people that I care about them by what I do. Actions speak louder than words.
- Enjoy it, use it, or put up with it.
- What you need to know is right in front of you.
- I tell it like I see it.
- I value my autonomy and flexibility. If any rules interfere with that, I'll usually just ignore them.
- I like school, but I would enjoy it more if we could change the daily routine. It's boring to always know what is coming next.
- I got into trouble in school for talking and moving around a lot. To this day, I have a hard time sitting still.
- My style of organization is my own. For example, it's hard for me to use someone else's filing system.
- I'm impulsive, and I have a hard time listening to advice from others.
- Everything I do is fun. If it isn't fun, I probably will not do it.
- I don't worry about the future. I deal with stuff when it happens.
- Often I do what I do to get reactions from others. It makes life more interesting.
- I tend to jump into the deep end of the pool without thinking.
- I'm like the Energizer Bunny: I keep going and going.
- Sitting still wears me out. If I sit still for ten minutes, I fall asleep. When I hit the bed at night, I immediately fall asleep.
- I am at my best in a crisis. Sometimes if there is no crisis, I will create one.
- I tend to put everything off to the last minute.
- I'm in constant motion. I need to move.

- When looking at a tree, it is not so much like seeing the tree as a whole but seeing every leaf, all the shades of green, the shapes of the leaves, the texture and details of the bark.
- I usually know the time of day, within a few minutes, without using a watch. I guess I notice environmental cues like shadows or the angle of the sun.
- In choosing a career, I find I need to actually experience it by watching a video, going to a job site, or even trying it out. A written job description does not interest me or provide the information I need. It is not tangible enough.
- I get a lot of joy and energy from little things: flowers, clouds, smells. No detail is too small to be a potential source of excitement and delight.
- I can give you directions to all sorts of places quite easily. I can tell you how many trees you'll pass and the color of the roof on the house at the corner.
- My closet is organized by color. If something is not in the right place, color-wise, I have to move it because it is not pleasing to my eye.
- I just could not do the workshop exercise. The colors of the objects we were working with clashed. It was too distracting.
- I have never liked tomatoes. However, every so often I have to try one. Since each time it is a new experience, I just might like them that day.
- I cannot sit still if something is going on. Open space schooling was very difficult for me. I couldn't tune out the activities that were happening all around. I heard everything that was going on in the classrooms next to mine, and they often sounded as if they were doing something more exciting than we were doing.
- I have never needed to return a clothing purchase because of a hole or defect. I notice it in the store before I buy it.
- I rarely need to buy a drink when I go out. I always know someone or soon will. Before the night is over, I'll know almost everyone.
- Often, if someone is wearing clothing that clashes, I find it very distracting and cannot concentrate on what the person is saying.

VIGNETTES

Scenes from the world of Extraverted Sensing

- If I'm boating with friends, I'll be the one who is really enjoying the moment. I will be talking to everyone, feeling the wind, hearing the sea gulls, jumping in the water to see how it feels.

- In a "type-alike" group exercise that involves describing an object, our group is usually the first to finish or will divert into other activities before any other group. There is only so much concrete data in a simple object. When you finish saying how the object looks, feels, smells, sounds, and tastes, you are done. There is nothing more to describe.

- Visiting an art gallery with friends, I realized that no one else saw the details in the artwork that I noticed immediately. In a painting of a house, for example, I saw the tiny key in the door. My friends had not noticed it and were amazed that I had. On the other hand, I can't remember what I wore yesterday and have only a vague recollection of what I did.

- I like to smell, touch, taste, or even listen to produce before buying. To decide whether fruit and vegetables are fresh and ripe, I tap on watermelons, smell cantaloupes, and taste grapes. I usually prefer to determine whether milk or food in the refrigerator is fresh by smell rather than reading the expiration date.

- I can go back somewhere after being away for years and negotiate the streets effortlessly. However, if some key feature has been changed, I get confused and lost. I navigate by landmarks or objects, never street names. I visit my daughter every week. One day I drove past her street. I had to turn around and go back. For ten years, without knowing it, I knew where to turn because of a mailbox on the corner that was made from an old stove. When it was removed, I just drove right by her street without realizing it. In a restaurant, it's difficult to order from reading the menu. I often order based upon seeing or smelling food from another table: "I'll have what that guy is having."

- After an exercise involving the use of apples, the virtually identical apples were collected and mixed together. A man with a preference for Extraverted Sensing was able to instantly pick out not only his apple but those of the people on either side of him as well.

At a wedding, I could not eat for fear that I might miss something. I had to be up walking around and talking to people. I only knew four people when I arrived. By the end of the reception, I knew almost everyone. I was even invited back to the house with the family, for the opening of the presents.

GIFTS

Unique strengths of Extraverted Sensing

- Accurate, objective, and detailed observation of a wide range of experiences in the current environment
- Enjoyment of life
- Can see all sides of an issue
- An aptitude for hands-on work
- Extremely reliable visual perception
- A talent for teaching others, by example, to smell the roses
- A knack for bringing excitement and life to any group
- Realism and practicality

CHAPTER 5

INTROVERTED SENSING (Si)

In this chapter, we seek to present a picture of the "pure" Introverted Sensing that we would see if we could carefully remove it from its natural state where it is influenced and colored by all the other elements of personality. Though no process actually exists separated from the rest of the personality, the portrait that follows reflects core characteristics that are in play whenever Introverted Sensing is engaged at a conscious level.

Introverted Sensing most clearly resembles the descriptions in the following pages when it is in the dominant (first) position. In fact, these descriptions are based on input from people for whom the process is dominant (ISTJ and ISFJ). But even with Introverted Sensing in the first position, what you observe will vary noticeably depending on other factors—particularly whether it is paired up with Extraverted Thinking or Extraverted Feeling in the auxiliary (second) position.

In order to draw a complete picture of the "essence" of Introverted Sensing, one must use bits and pieces that cannot individually demonstrate "pure" Si. Like the splashes of color in an impressionist painting, however, the bullets in this chapter, when taken all together, reveal a vivid portrait that will enable you to recognize Introverted Sensing when you see it. Knowing what the process would look like if it could be separated from other influences is the foundation of process watching, the practice that will quickly take you as far as you want to go in understanding personality.

Introverted Sensing is an information-gathering process. It focuses on the subjective, internal world of past experience by comparing current sensory experiences to similar past experiences through a vivid and detailed internal database of memories. Si wants to relive the past and selectively explore the impact and significance of current events, people, and experiences.

**Dominant for
ISTJ and ISFJ**

**Auxiliary for
ESTJ and ESFJ**

KEY FEATURES
Introverted Sensing

- Experiences the present world through comparison with previous experiences.
- Re-experiences the past sequentially, in vivid sensory detail.
- Focuses on the memories and comparisons that are triggered by current objects, people, and events.
- Stores sensory references from the past in a subjective internal database.
- Has a high level of internal body awareness.
- Subjectively selects what gets noticed in the present and recalled from the past.
- Seeks to use previous experience as a guide for exploring the current experience.

WHAT'S GOING ON?
Introverted Sensing

- Sees the current world through subjective internal filters.
- Uses an external stimulus in the present to stimulate an internal experience: the recall of the past.
- Asks: How does this event in the present compare to similar events in the past? What is different? What is the same? How can it be improved?
- Resembles a mental Rolodex file, video, or database for sorting through the internal images to find the right reference.
- Enables accurate recall of all steps or events in the exact order in which they happened.
- Looks at what happened and how it could be improved. Learns from past mistakes.
- Is energized through combining vivid past experiences with the present to relive special moments.

When people are using their preferred Introverted Sensing

- Their past experience provides the frame of reference for comparison with their present experience.
- Much attention is paid to the facts and details of personally significant past experiences and how they are similar to or different from the present experience.

- Their memories are clear and detailed but subjective, so they will not necessarily agree with someone else's recollection of the same events.

- Their most vivid memories are those that were most impactful. These memories are replayed over and over again with all the associated details and emotions. It is like actually physically reliving the event and re-experiencing the same emotions.

- They prefer and trust their subjective recall. They may simply ignore someone else's conflicting version of events and rigidly defend their own. Accepting a different version would require changing the memory itself. It would be like re-recording the whole event.

- They are usually closely attuned to the physical condition and energy of their bodies.

- The current experience that is triggering a recollection may be integrated with the memory, or it may be virtually ignored if found to be not relevant to the memory.

- They may form associations with people or things in the present, based on someone or something similar from the past.

- The intensity of a previous experience determines what will be remembered. Watching a sunset does not bring to mind every sunset ever seen, just the significant ones. These could include the best sunset ever or ones associated with significant events like falling in love or the death of a loved one.

- They are referencing an internal database that is filled with an enormous amount of detail. The detail, however, is not 100 percent reliable as an objective record of the experience or event.

- Familiarity has a great impact on making a current event more comfortable because the more similar the event is to past ones, the more easily it can be compared to them internally.

- No one can change the internal references except the individual.

- The current data and experience are not real until they have been validated by comparison with a similar circumstance or experience.

- The recollection of a past event is automatically and immediately overlaid on the current experience.

- They interpret the current situation through association with previous experiences. Sometimes this produces brilliant insights. Often it gives them a surprisingly complete grasp of the current situation. Occasionally it leads to misinterpretation and erroneous assumptions.

- A smell or sound can trigger a flood of vivid memories, with all of the related emotions.
- The present stimulus can be disregarded and reliving the past can become the current experience.
- Their internal experience is about the most memorable one of its kind, whether good or bad, happy or sad.
- They may appear quiet and composed, while internally they are very active, perhaps even in turmoil.
- When something happens that is different from anything that they have personally experienced before, they need to find something that is similar in some way so it can be used for comparison.
- What is important to them is the subjective experience, not the present external event.
- They tend to do familiar activities well. Their internalized experiences, along with their ability to evaluate and compare them, serve as a reference library of best practices.
- They cannot be pressured into changing a memory. Creating it was very personal and vivid. Recreating it must be done independently as well.
- Remembered information is reality to them. Revising a memory is not just a matter of altering a record of an experience. It is like changing the experience itself.

FROM THE OUTSIDE, LOOKING IN

When we experience people who are engaging their preferred Introverted Sensing, they

- Do not always seem to be with us in the present. Sometimes, when they return from their reverie, they tell a story from their past that seems especially important to them.
- Seem to recall past events from a unique perspective. The specific details and emphasis are strongly colored by how they personally experienced the event.
- Tell about an event as a sequential, personal story. It is not like a "report," in which one seeks to summarize the key objective facts of what happened and may make a point or reach a conclusion. Their reason for telling the story seems to be in the telling itself.

- Sometimes reject new information that might cause them to change their course of action.
- Are often predictable in their actions.
- Usually are well organized and neat.
- Are clear and confident about knowing what to do in any given setting or situation based on their prior experience.
- May show emotional behavior even when there is nothing in the current external environment to support or explain that emotion.
- May approach a task with statements such as "We did something like this before and it was not successful. This part worked but that part didn't. Here is how we can make it work better this time."
- Often describe tangible items by comparison to other objects. They frequently use phrases that start with "looks like," "seems like," "feels like," and "tastes like."
- Often compare events and situations to ones from the past. You may hear "I've seen this before" or "that reminds me of the time."
- Understand concrete descriptions and stories that make a point through comparisons.
- Can get sidetracked into talking about topics that are related to the subject at hand rather than talking about the subject itself.
- May seem to wander aimlessly through stories of questionable relevance as they search their internal database for the correct one to use for comparison. Sometimes it is difficult for others to listen patiently to them while they sort it out.
- May recount previous events in great detail. Sometimes only the storytellers themselves can see how those events are relevant to what is going on now.
- Can bring great insight to a situation through their past experiences.
- May go back and forth between two extremes of energy during a conversation. They could become animated and energetic if the subject evokes either happy or sad memories. On the other hand, they could show no interest at all if the subject is not something they have personally experienced.
- May not provide much input or feedback during group decision making unless allowed time to access their internal world.
- Can usually tell you exactly what you said at a specific time. If you disagree with them about what you said, they may become rigid in defending their recollection or totally shut down and not communicate at all.

- May be difficult to get to know.
- Often have great confidence and certainty about the right way to do tasks.
- Tend to be dependable and stable.
- Have a learning style that is like rolling a carpet forward: linear, with each new learning an extension of the previous one.
- Usually cannot be convinced that they are not recalling facts accurately. The more they are pressured or coerced, the more resistant they become. They need to be allowed to decide for themselves whether their internal data is incorrect and given space to re-form their memory.
- Tend to accept change more easily when they can look to a similar transition in the past and find support for making the change in order to correct mistakes or improve a situation.

CONTRIBUTIONS

Special perspectives and approaches of Introverted Sensing

- Internal structure and organization for any task, project, or group
- Development of effective solutions based on past experience
- Lessons learned from previous mistakes
- Institutional memory and a sense of organizational continuity through a history of past successes and failures
- An internal template for how familiar tasks are done and how to build from experience to approach new tasks
- A high level of precise internal body awareness
- A calm and professional manner
- Insightfulness, usually without unnecessary assertiveness

FROM THE INSIDE

Paraphrased descriptions of what it is like to gather information through one's preferred Introverted Sensing

- Experience is like constant déjà vu. Everyone occasionally has the experience of some sight or smell instantly transporting them to a vivid recollection of a past event, but for me it's almost constant. It is where I live.

- My internal data is a lot like having detailed photographic plates that are available to me as a clear series of sequential pictures.
- It's like a movie or video in my head that replays all the details over and over.
- It's like a slide show or a mental Rolodex. The images always come to me in a certain order. These images are superimposed over what is going on in the present environment, which allows me to see all the similarities and differences.
- I relive the experience. I feel exactly what I felt before, just as intensely.
- I never use a camera because my internal pictures are so much more vivid and rich. Photographs are too flat and lifeless. The pictures inside are what really bring me back to a time and place.
- I know the day's weather by looking at the sky and comparing it to the pictures of skies in my memory and remembering the weather we had on those days.
- Once I identify something, there's usually no need to personally experience it any further. I get only what I need to trigger the relevant images.
- I'm hesitant to embark on totally new ventures. I am much more comfortable when I have already experienced something similar.
- I am the only one who can revise a memory. Changing a memory is like destroying a valued object, like shattering a glass picture. It is done only when new additions to my internal database absolutely require revising the old material. Then I have to rebuild the memory from scratch.
- I am very good at knowing when something is not right with my body. Without thinking about it I constantly and automatically compare my internal readings, like heart rate, pain, and energy level, with their normal state. I can usually tell if something is wrong with me long before any doctor or medical test can pick it up.
- I don't like a lot of change.
- If you talk to me about something I have not personally experienced, I may just blank out. I do not have a clue what you're talking about because I don't have a reference.
- I can recall in extreme detail the room layouts of places I have been. In department stores, my friends are amazed by how I can go to the exact location where we saw an item several weeks before.

- I enjoy shocking people by describing what they wore and what they said in a meeting ten years ago.
- I can describe, in great detail, several scenes and events that happened when I was very young.
- I remember a lot about when I was sick as a child, even the clothes that my parents were wearing. I was nine months old when I was sick, and I can still recall the experience fifty years later.
- I really hate driving somewhere I've never been before. When I do get directions, I prefer to get specific details such as mileage or landmarks to go by. Maps don't work well for me. Once I've been somewhere, I normally stick with the same route that I know.
- In choosing a career, I needed to reflect upon what had worked and not worked for me before and what I had liked and not liked in previous jobs.
- Whenever I drink a beer, I'm comparing it to my memory of the "perfect" beer. Every beer I ever taste is compared to that beer. If I ever taste one that's better, I'll know it with certainty, and that will become my new standard of the perfect beer.
- I can remember every teacher I ever had. I can hear their voices, picture the classrooms, and remember most of my classmates and what we did.

VIGNETTES

Scenes from the world of Introverted Sensing

- A participant in a four-day workshop was able to describe in exact detail what each of the thirty-four participants had worn each day. She could also cross-reference those internal images and knew which people had worn the same articles twice.
- I experience a tree by overlaying that tree with memories of significant trees from the past. When I am looking at a tree, it could bring up pleasant childhood memories of a tree with a swing or maybe unpleasant memories of getting stuck in a tree. I'm sure that no one else would experience that same tree in the same way that I do because my past associations with trees are mine alone.
- If you bump into an old acquaintance with a preference for Introverted Sensing, your acquaintance may well proceed to tell you the details of your last encounter: where you were, what you were wearing, the

weather, and what you talked about. He or she may make comparisons between the two meetings, such as noting changes in your hair style.

- In a restaurant, I'll remember what I ate there before or what I had at a similar restaurant. My menu selection will be based on this previous experience. If the menu choices are so completely strange to me that useful internal comparisons cannot be found, the waiter can be helpful by giving me something familiar to work with: by talking about the spices or the method of preparation or by comparing the menu items to the dishes that I know.

- In a scene with friends on a boat, I'll probably be drifting off in my mind to another boat ride. I'll be reliving what was happening, whom I was with, where we went, and what we saw.

- In a "type-alike" group exercise that focuses on talking about an object, our group always includes memories triggered by, and usually closely associated with, the object. For example, when a bag of eight markers was provided for the exercise, we remembered working with sets of markers in the past. Of course, we also knew that there should have been ten markers in the set and which colors were missing.

- While planning with some business associates where to go for dinner, one young man said he wanted to go somewhere that served spareribs. He proceeded to tell us about a place in his hometown that served "the best ribs in the world." As he was describing them, he came alive. His face became animated and he even began salivating. He said that he could actually taste the ribs. The others in the group were pulled into his experience by his vivid descriptions and his energy. But when he was done reliving the memory of those ribs, he no longer wanted ribs for dinner. He said that he had just experienced the best ribs in the world and any others would be a disappointment.

- My young nephew walked through the door and immediately wanted to know what happened to the rug in front of the door. Since I had removed the old rug a while ago, I didn't immediately understand the question, so I asked, "What rug?" Taking my question as my not valuing his memory, he got angry, put his hands on his hips, stomped his foot, and said, "You know, the green rug that was right here!" After I apologized and explained what had happened to it, he felt validated. He proceeded to compare the new rug with the old rug.

A woman described her vacation to Cancun. As she talked, her facial expression changed. She was talking about how much she had enjoyed herself. She said she could smell the Cancun air, see the fish in the clear water, feel the breeze on her face, and hear the birds. She said she immediately had the same sense of relaxation she had while in Cancun.

GIFTS

Unique strengths of Introverted Sensing

- Awareness of when something is out of place, whether it is an object in a room or a step in a process, by comparison to a remembered internal image of the same environment or procedure
- Learn from past experience, to rarely make the same mistake twice
- A reliable knowledge of the steps, in sequence, involved in most events or projects
- Lend substance to the current situation by providing historical context
- Bring structure to the current task or situation based upon what has or has not worked before
- Careful attention to detail
- Detailed, vivid memory
- Stability

CHAPTER 6

EXTRAVERTED INTUITING (Ne)

In this chapter, we seek to present a picture of the "pure" Extraverted Intuiting that we would see if we could carefully remove it from its natural state where it is influenced and colored by all the other elements of personality. Though no process actually exists separated from the rest of the personality, the portrait that follows reflects core characteristics that are in play whenever Extraverted Intuiting is engaged at a conscious level.

Extraverted Intuiting most clearly resembles the descriptions in the following pages when it is in the dominant (first) position. In fact, these descriptions are based on input from people for whom the process is dominant (ENTP and ENFP). But even with Extraverted Intuiting in the first position, what you observe will vary noticeably depending on other factors—particularly whether it is paired up with Introverted Thinking or Introverted Feeling in the auxiliary (second) position.

In order to draw a complete picture of the "essence" of Extraverted Intuiting, one must use bits and pieces that cannot individually demonstrate "pure" Ne. Like the splashes of color in an impressionist painting, however, the bullets in this chapter, when taken all together, reveal a vivid portrait that will enable you to recognize Extraverted Intuiting when you see it. Knowing what the process would look like if it could be separated from other influences is the foundation of process watching, the practice that will quickly take you as far as you want to go in understanding personality.

Extraverted Intuiting is an information-gathering process. It focuses on the objective, external world to find substantive connections and relationships between the objects, people, and events in the environment. Ne wants to generate real-world possibilities.

**Dominant for
ENTP and ENFP**

**Auxiliary for
INTP and INFP**

KEY FEATURES
Extraverted Intuiting

- Is driven to build future possibilities from the objective data in the environment.
- Explores what could be.
- Has an external focus that spans the past, present, and future.
- Sees the patterns and connections that shape future alternatives.
- Forms a series of verifiable links that create patterns and possibilities.
- Almost instantaneously creates an entire realm of specific possibilities.
- Seeks a broad understanding of the global picture based on the present external situation.

WHAT'S GOING ON?
Extraverted Intuiting

- Detects emerging possibilities in the information, events, and objects in the environment.
- Focuses on concrete possibilities in the environments of the present and future.
- Leaps from one data point to another, in no apparent order, to find connection.
- Looks at everything in the context of its relationships and associations with other information, events, and objectives.
- Gathers information in clusters. Nothing stands by itself, discrete and unconnected.
- May take in information selectively, according to its relevance to the current inspiration.
- Is about "connecting the dots."
- Envisions how situations, objects, and information can be used.
- Connects the current world to future possibilities and options.
- Is triggered by the external world.

When people are using their preferred Extraverted Intuiting

- The starting point is always information or options taken from the external environment.

- Their learning style is nonlinear.

  Their awareness of concrete information or situations in the present pulses in and out as new data creates a stream of connections. Each check-in for data is quickly followed by a journey in pursuit of new possibilities; then they check in for additional data and take off again with more possibilities.

- They are exploring the potential that is embedded within every fact, situation, person, or object.

- The series of associations connected to the information is what creates the possibilities.

  Generating more and more possibilities is their goal. The value of the possibilities is not important. Usually no editing occurs.

  Knowledge expands outward from each piece of information.

  They are asking, "What new things could be done with . . . ?"

- The possibilities that they see are imagined versions of the tangible world. Though based firmly in verifiable reality, these ideas often lack specific concrete details.

- They are creating opportunities by understanding what can happen.

- New enterprises are exciting because they are full of possibilities.

- The methodology of brainstorming comes very naturally, and they use it easily and effectively.

- They excel at creating new ways of doing old tasks.

- They want to change what is to what could be. They have a need to transform existing information by exploring the widest possible range of possibilities.

- They tend to spin off ideas in a spontaneous, unstructured way.

- A global picture appears effortlessly and almost instantaneously to them.

FROM THE OUTSIDE, LOOKING IN

When we experience people who are engaging their preferred Extraverted Intuiting, they

- Can suddenly gush with unexpected enthusiasm because their energy comes from generating and pursuing possibilities that appear spontaneously to them.

- May drop current, unfinished projects in the excitement of discovering a new possibility. There is a danger that this can become a lifestyle.
- Can be indecisive. Too many possibilities can make choices difficult.
- May listen to others just long enough to start generating connections.
- Seem to get sidetracked a lot. In a data-gathering task, for example, they may be quickly distracted by the possibilities suggested to them by the data.
- Usually express themselves effortlessly, especially when dealing with new ideas and possibilities.
- Sometimes seem compelled to assert their independence.
- Are quickly bored by stable conditions. Without new possibilities, they may even feel trapped.
- Usually connect easily with people.
- May get frustrated and annoyed with those who cannot see the big picture or the connections and possibilities of what could happen.
- Are open-minded. They are always willing to change theories or switch gears as new information comes in.
- Can seem to be quite powerful when they are promoting an idea, then seem flighty the next moment as they jump from that idea to another and then to another.
- Are often seen as being very quick of mind because they assimilate, connect, and use new information so rapidly.
- Are interested in everything. It can be hard for others to know how to deal with someone who is interested in everything.
- Usually end up doing what seems most compelling to them—whatever catches their attention—even if it means giving short shrift to a longstanding commitment.
- Like to teach people new ways to look at everything.
- Have the hardest time with people who are closed-minded. People who are not willing to consider new ideas are difficult for them to deal with.
- Love change for the sake of change. Anything new and different is exciting.

CONTRIBUTIONS

Special perspectives and approaches of Extraverted Intuiting

- Imagining new scenarios and suggest multiple options
- An entrepreneurial spirit
- Brainstorming skills
- Diagnostic abilities
- A talent for evaluating potential
- A knack for approaching questions by developing working hypotheses
- Enlist people to enthusiastically support their projects
- Networking

FROM THE INSIDE

Paraphrased descriptions of what it is like to gather information through one's preferred Extraverted Intuiting

- I love the rush of finding a new approach, a new concept, or a new idea. Work is play, but it has to be creative. Routine equals boredom.
- Every time I near closure, I come up with a new possibility.
- I'm a juggler at heart. I always have several balls in the air at once.
- It's not so much about seeing what is there as seeing the connections between what is there. I can almost see a picture of the connections. I see things collectively rather than literally or in detail.
- My life can sometimes seem like an endless series of new, often un-completed, projects.
- We could do this, or maybe that, or maybe this other thing.
- My conclusion or decision is never final, just the current best option.
- Trying to explain to others how situation A connects to B and C and so on can be frustrating. Most people won't understand it or believe it. Often, I don't even try to explain.
- Change is an opportunity. I like to take risks.
- I have lots of good friends.
- Making mistakes is not a big deal. I take the best approach I can think of and always learn something, regardless of whether or not it succeeds. Not daring to risk failure—that would be a terrible way to live.
- I thrive on change.

- My pace wears out a lot of people.
- I usually read five or six books at once.
- My personal spaces at home and at work may appear disorganized, but I know where everything is.
- I'm always ready to turn on a dime.
- When I'm generating possibilities, I'm physically engaged. It's an active sport.
- I sometimes feel that I'm missing out on enjoying the present.
- Sometimes I'm so far ahead of myself in the future that I don't allow myself to experience the moment.
- I can't stand tasks always being done the same way. How are you ever going to know if you can improve something if you don't change it?
- I need to really inspire you and have you really enjoy it, or I've failed.
- I respect people who listen and try to understand all the information and who will try different options. I am a risk taker and like to be with people who take risks.
- I'm still searching for what I want to be when I grow up.
- I'm always asking myself, How can I use this new information?
- The moment I get new information, I'm generating a brand-new array of options.
- Almost instantly as I take in new or modified information, a new array of connections and options is built upon the old.
- I see a series of links rapidly appearing, each connecting to the next, with no gaps. It's very much like the way a computer operates.
- I like to view everything as if from thirty-five thousand feet overhead. I enjoy seeing how all the pieces fit together.
- All the pieces go together in a distinct pattern as in a kaleidoscope. But the moment the smallest change occurs, then like a tap on the kaleidoscope, the individual pieces all bump each other around into an entirely new pattern.
- I love to see my ideas come to fruition, but I'd rather have someone else be the one to do that part.
- Just feed me information and I go off like a rocket with endless possibilities. Everyone else just needs to get out of the way. Even if I'm not aimed right, I will get there eventually.

Brainstorming is always exciting. Everyone is engaged. Things are really happening!

Passively receiving information, as in a lecture, is very hard. I need to discuss. I am interested in how the new information changes everything else. I always ask a lot of questions.

I'm at my best in the midst of confusion. Sorting through an overabundance of options is what I do all the time anyway.

The fun is in figuring it out—whatever it is. What are the options and possibilities hidden within the confusion?

The conventional approach holds no attraction for me. Coming up with an innovative solution is what gets me excited.

It's almost as if I have a carousel in my mind that is constantly spinning and throwing off ideas as it spins.

Attempting to collect information in a structured way is uncomfortable for me. It's too constraining.

I usually use option exploration as a basic team-building tool.

Whatever it is, I try to change it.

I often find myself imagining specific future events, like the day my daughter will get her driver's license, become president, or have my grandchildren. If nothing is going on to stimulate me, I will create possibilities out of my imagination.

I'm thinking of moving just for a change of scene.

You can pretty much get me to try anything at least once.

In choosing careers, the key for me is to explore possibilities while keeping options open. Rather than choosing a job, I need to design a career path. The ideal career for me is one that could lead in several different directions to a wide array of job options in the future.

When we go out, I'm great at suggesting what we could do. But don't ask me to choose. I don't enjoy making the decision because that would also be a decision to not do all the other possible choices.

Generating possibilities is the fun part. Choosing from among them reduces the options, so I tend to keep gathering information and generating options rather than moving on to decision making.

I have a garage overflowing with salvaged junk because I see all sorts of projects that could be done with it.

I like to have several balls in the air at once. The challenge of the juggling is really what I'm all about. The more possibilities I see, the more enthused I become; and the more enthused I become, the more possibilities I think of.

VIGNETTES

Scenes from the world of Extraverted Intuiting

In a board meeting, some sales numbers might be presented and I will immediately launch into possibilities: "We should roll out our new product line early" or "We can save on shipping if we do this." Maybe the presenter wasn't even finished. If she or he continues with more information, I may go off again with a whole new set of ideas and possibilities. This can blow people away if they're not used to it.

My grandson loves checkers for the possibilities they offer. He invents an endless variety of games to play with the board and checkers. I cannot remember the last time we played a game of regular checkers.

My wife was trying to describe what she wanted our new house to look like. All she could talk about was having everything designed so that we would be able to build on additions or rooms in the future. It took her two years to even put anything specific down on paper.

My Extraverted Intuiting husband will suddenly start talking about more possibilities when I thought we'd made a decision hours ago.

When I look at a tree, I see the possibilities inherent in the tree. I may picture a playhouse that could be built in the tree. I might envision how the playhouse could be decorated, events happening there, kids playing or relaxing, parties, games, and so on.

At a restaurant, my challenge is to make choices from among all the enticing possibilities. I'm thinking, maybe I'll have this, but that looks good too. I often suggest that we order different dishes and share. I almost always go last so I can make sure I get something that is different from what everyone else orders.

If I am relaxing on a boat with friends, I may actually be considering options for dinner: where we will go and what we will do tonight, tomorrow, next week. I'm relaxing by drifting with the possibilities. It's not the boat, the water, or the sunshine that I enjoy so much as the opportunity to talk to my friends about ideas and possibilities for the future. Even planning future boat excursions is fun.

- In a "type-alike" group exercise involving an object, our group worked together to come up with possibilities of what could be done with the object. We could have gone on talking for days since the possibilities were virtually infinite.

- After two months of checking and rechecking to be sure that my family agreed that we should sell our piano, I finally had the dealer come and take it away. When my Extraverted Intuiting husband and daughter came home, they were both shocked that I had made such a major decision without them. They had assumed that selling it was just one option among many and that the discussion would continue indefinitely.

GIFTS

Unique strengths of Extraverted Intuiting

- Ingenious at coming up with possible solutions
- Filling in the blanks with people, objects, or events by connecting all the known information into explanations that fit
- Perception on a global scale
- A knack for serving as a bridge between people, connecting their ideas and looking at alternative scenarios
- Teaching people new ways of looking at everything
- A flair for presenting something familiar in a new and compelling way that induces people to rally in support
- Open-mindedness
- A talent for creating options and opportunities

CHAPTER 7

INTROVERTED INTUITING (Ni)

In this chapter, we seek to present a picture of the "pure" Introverted Intuiting that we would see if we could carefully remove it from its natural state where it is influenced and colored by all the other elements of personality. Though no process actually exists separated from the rest of the personality, the portrait that follows reflects core characteristics that are in play whenever Introverted Intuiting is engaged at a conscious level.

Introverted Intuiting most clearly resembles the descriptions in the following pages when it is in the dominant (first) position. In fact, these descriptions are based on input from people for whom the process is dominant (INTJ and INFJ). But even with Introverted Intuiting in the first position, what you observe will vary noticeably depending on other factors—particularly whether it is paired up with Extraverted Thinking or Extraverted Feeling in the auxiliary (second) position.

In order to draw a complete picture of the "essence" of Introverted Intuiting, one must use bits and pieces that cannot individually demonstrate "pure" Ni. Like the splashes of color in an impressionist painting, however, the bullets in this chapter, when taken all together, reveal a vivid portrait that will enable you to recognize Introverted Intuiting when you see it. Knowing what the process would look like if it could be separated from other influences is the foundation of process watching, the practice that will quickly take you as far as you want to go in understanding personality.

Introverted Intuiting is an information-gathering process. It focuses on the subjective, internal world of the unconscious to find intangible connections and abstract relationships between the contents of the unconscious and/or the environment. Ni wants to discover underlying significance, systems, and meaning.

**Dominant for
INTJ and INFJ**

**Auxiliary for
ENTJ and ENFJ**

KEY FEATURES

Introverted Intuiting

- Focuses on the contents of the unconscious.
- Involves a psychic awareness of the intangible.
- Searches for grand patterns, themes, and systems in order to understand the meaning and significance of everything.
- Operates unpredictably, often through flashes of insight.
- Seeks to understand through an abstract sense of the essential nature of all things and their complex interrelationships.
- Attaches meaning and symbolism to the concrete world of the senses.
- Seeks to understand the entire "dance of the universe."

WHAT'S GOING ON?

Introverted Intuiting

- Is the only perception process that is independent of the conscious mind.
- Is the only process that does not need any external stimulus.
- Can be triggered either internally or externally or have no identifiable trigger at all.
- Works in mysterious ways and on its own timetable.
- Views everything on the broadest, most complex level possible.
- Has an abstract, futuristic approach to information.
- Asks, "What else is going on here?"
- Quickly grasps the meaning behind words. Its focus is on reading between the lines.
- Is the keeper of the so-called sixth sense. Unexplainable information can take the form of hunches, clairvoyance, abstract intuition, and messages from the unconscious.
- Is really ultimately about trying to understand life itself.

When people are using their preferred Introverted Intuiting

- Unconscious images are as real to them as anything tangible.
- An external object is important primarily for what it may release within them.

- They can intentionally access the process only by creating certain conditions and letting it happen.
- That which can be perceived by the five senses is important mainly as a source of clues to aid in the pursuit of an inner understanding of the universal truths that the tangible objects represent.
- They look for associations and connections to identify patterns and systems in order to see and understand everything at once as an interconnected whole.
- The focus is on indistinct, broad-stroke futures, with seemingly little regard for apparent factual inconsistencies.
- Details are not viewed as being very interesting or important.
- Gathering concrete information is a challenge. They tend to move quickly, sometimes prematurely, into internal abstractions.
- An understanding of what is beneath the surface comes easily.
- The connections that they perceive are often not demonstrable. Often these connections appear to others to be leaps or gaps but are actually links of abstract knowing, possibly through pattern recognition.
- Life is about inner images: abstractions and visions of how things are and how they could be.
- They view everything in the tangible world as a reflection of the much more complex and interesting world "behind the curtain."
- They seek to understand complexity through its simple underlying essence.
- Visions and intuitive insights are trusted and valued. They "just know" with a confidence and certainty that often cannot be justified or explained to others.
- They view abstract relationships as real and vague future scenarios as actual alternate futures. People who dispute their predictions simply lack the vision to be able to see what is coming.
- Inspiration is the driver, the energizer, and the goal.
- They are carrying on a search for meaning: a search for the cosmic significance and for the underlying commonalities of all that we see.

FROM THE OUTSIDE, LOOKING IN

When we experience people who are engaging their preferred Introverted Intuiting, they

- Can be difficult to relate to or understand. The unconscious nature of their process is very different from the other three approaches to Perceiving. Not only are their perceptions unique to the individual, but they are nearly impossible to explain or describe in words.
- May experience insights that are not connected to the tangible world in any way that makes sense to anyone else.
- Tend to search for a better solution, even if the current one works just fine. They are always looking for something new and unlike anything else. They do not want to hear "if it ain't broke, don't fix it" because they believe that everything can be reinvented and improved.
- May be seen as "way out there." In the most dramatic cases they may be called shamans, prophets, or visionaries if other people's reactions are positive. Negative responses can get them labeled as crackpots, radicals, or witches. The difference depends not so much upon the contents of their visions as on how those visions are expressed and whether or not others are receptive to their messages.
- Usually have little concern about the usefulness of their insights.
- Sometimes are seen as inconsistent or even disloyal. Their internal integrity is complex and private and may not be apparent to others.
- Often communicate through abstractions, metaphors, images, and symbols.
- Can sound halting, rambling, or awkward as they search for words that convey their abstract thoughts.
- Must create brand-new imagery and language every time they attempt to explain anything since they are trying to express something that comes from a place where perception is outside the bounds of language.
- May fall into ever-more vague and theoretical language as they try to explain something, prove something, or convince you.
- Often communicate very little specific concrete data and sometimes none at all. The outer world of tangible facts may have little to do with the validity of the message they are trying to convey.
- May use abstract or symbolic art as a way of communicating.

- Have no limits on the scope of their perception except for the challenges of describing it to others.
- Have a hard time listening carefully for long. They are too preoccupied with searching for the meaning and patterns behind the words.
- Have a very future-oriented focus on what may come to pass.
- Seem to make everything more complex. To them, when you look beneath the surface, all things are interconnected and are, indeed, incredibly complex.
- Are sometimes slow to reply. They are not usually seen as being quick on their feet. Before responding, they usually need time to access internal information and consider how it fits in with the rest of the universe. At other times they may be too quick to reply because the information they present with such conviction is so far removed from the immediate subject being discussed that it sounds like an off-the-wall comment.
- May seem to change their focus in a split second from talking about bits of information to making a dramatically broad general statement about what is really going on.
- May tune out conversations that do not have meaning or depth for them.
- Often ask questions that are very penetrating and may be uncomfortable for others.
- Like to ask why. If asked and answered enough times, the question brings them to the depth of understanding that is of interest to them.
- Want to know what is really going on behind the facade.
- Are extremely independent and take pride in that.
- Have little regard for authority. They decide for themselves whether or not rules and regulations make sense and should be followed.
- Tend to be exceptionally stubborn.
- Have difficulty accepting limitations and constraints. They really believe that the impossible usually just takes a little longer. If you want to see them take action, tell them they cannot do something.
- Are easily bored by repetitive tasks unless a task requires so little attention that it allows them to focus on their internal world.
- Are hard to fully challenge.
- May appear arrogant.
- Are often quiet in their demeanor. They may even be awkward and shy.

- Can become very vocal, passionate, animated, and obstinate when they are convinced that they understand something that others need to know.
- Can appear moody or preoccupied. They are often "off somewhere" internally. Their outward demeanor usually reflects what is going on inside, which may be out of sync with what is happening around them.
- May have difficulty sharing their creativity with others.
- Are often seen as daydreamers.
- Often excel at higher, more theoretical and abstract levels of education.

CONTRIBUTIONS
Special perspectives and approaches of Introverted Intuiting

- A fine-tuned awareness of people's authenticity level and of how safe it is to be open, honest, and vulnerable with them
- An understanding that all things are interrelated in ways that are often intangible and perhaps even unknowable
- Insight into what is going on beneath the surface through a sense of the meaning of what can be seen
- A talent for operating outside the box
- Applying metaphors and symbols
- Advancing scientific theory beyond the bounds of conventional wisdom
- A capacity to promote understanding by teaching the whys and wherefores
- The vision that guides strategic planning

FROM THE INSIDE
Paraphrased descriptions of what it is like to gather information through one's preferred Introverted Intuiting

- Sometimes I just know something. Even though I don't always understand how I know it, I'm certain that I'm right.
- I always wonder, What does this really mean?
- I will always accept input for consideration, but I can't be coerced.

- I want to understand how complex processes and mechanisms work. I love theory and abstract concepts. The more theoretical and abstract a conversation or line of thought is, the more exciting it is.
- I'm always being told to get my head out of the clouds and come down to earth.
- I am happy when I begin to understand what is going on, to see what will happen.
- I'm gratified when I see things happening as I said they would.
- I am more interested in pioneering a new road than exploring anything along the beaten path.
- I am deeply discontented with routine work that doesn't allow for inspiration or creativity.
- I get very frustrated and impatient when others cannot see what I see and will not listen to me. It seems that invariably, a while later someone else will say the same thing and then people will listen and think it is a great idea.
- In a "type-alike" group exercise focusing on an object, everyone in our group was disappointed that it wasn't something more complex or meaningful.
- The flash of inspiration comes when it wants to come. I can't consciously summon it.
- I get a sense of who people are very quickly. I have to remind myself that they probably don't know me as well as I know them.
- You have to search for the meaning in something. You sense the path, but you have to feel your way along it. It's mostly hazy, with a flash of clarity here and there. You think maybe you see something in the distance, but it is never clear. You move through the haze with the certainty that there is something out there to strive to reach. Exactly what that something is, you may never know.
- My best ideas come to me during my morning shower. I think I do my best thinking in the morning because I've had a chance to sleep on an idea.
- I always know about people.
- Sometimes it is hard to start a task. I need to wait for an understanding of the implications, nuances, and broad scope of it because only then will I know what I need to do and how to do it. People often tell me that I procrastinate.

- I usually don't remember people's names or factual information about them very well.

- I have lived in the same city most of my life. I don't think anyone is better at knowing the best route from one point to another in any given weather or traffic. On the other hand, I couldn't tell you the names of most of the streets.

- I was having dinner with a friend. Suddenly I had a clear picture in my mind of what would happen to her on her vacation. Sometimes I get flashes with a lot of information, and other times I have to reflect to figure out what a vision meant.

- I often feel like the child in the story "The Emperor's New Clothes." I am the only one who says what is really going on. I have learned that sometimes I need to hold myself back and not say it out loud.

- I am sometimes able to have a sense of what the future holds without anything in the external world appearing to support the prediction.

- I can sometimes feel people's pain when I look at or touch them.

- In finding a career, I know what I do not like, but it is hard to put together a clear vision of what I would like to do. What I do know is pretty vague, as in "I'd like to work with people, to work with my hands or work with animals, or to do work that has meaning."

- It's really frustrating when I know how something can be done more effectively and see people clinging to the old way.

- I do not let details and facts get in the way of solutions.

- I tend to get lost when navigating through the physical world. I guess I'm the classic absent-minded professor.

- I have a strong sense about danger. On several occasions I have ducked out of harm's way in the nick of time because I sensed it coming. Usually, though, it just comes through as a reliable sense of which situations to avoid.

- Until my fiftieth birthday, I had never really been surprised in my life. That party was the first time that I did not know about something ahead of time. As a child, I was never surprised at Christmas or birthdays. I knew what presents I would be getting.

- I feel as if I have about five hundred social studies in progress in my head at all times. Every behavior I observe gets automatically fed into those studies to continually revise my hypotheses about human nature and interaction.

VIGNETTES

Scenes from the world of Introverted Intuiting

When I am looking at a tree, I often don't really see the tree itself. I might be envisioning the forest as it was hundreds of years ago, with Indians living there, or seeing the earth being formed or the forest growing. I could be seeing the tree's environment in the future. I may go off onto an environmental tangent, pondering trees' contributions to the ecosystem or the future of the planet. I may explore a symbolic tangent: the tree as a symbol of life force or as a safe haven for animals.

In a restaurant, I'll probably be very aware of the atmosphere. I may not even pay much attention to the food but will usually tune in to the social dynamics between the people at the table. I'll ponder all sorts of questions: What is the occasion? Should we find a quiet corner where we can talk? What does it mean that we are gathered here together? Is there a special occasion to celebrate?

In a boat with friends, I'll be wondering: What is this trip really all about? Is everyone really saying what they mean? How does this all play out in the greater scheme? What impact will this boat ride have on our future relationships? I may not even notice the weather.

In a "type-alike" group exercise involving instructions to talk about a certain object, our group gravitates immediately to expansive images and themes. For example, one time the object was a simple paper bag. We had very little discussion. One man said, "Everything in the universe can fit into this bag." This statement was written on a piece of paper and placed in the bag. That was all that needed to be said. Everyone in the group then went off on their own internal journey in search of meaning.

GIFTS

Unique strengths of Introverted Intuiting

A capacity for seeing the shape of possible futures, unrestricted by time, place, concrete data, or events

Grasping the whole context in a flash of insight

A tendency to fill the roles of prophets and visionary leaders to inspire cultural change toward new models of what can be

- A talent for teaching a deeper level of understanding
- Connecting society to the intangible, metaphysical world (shamans)
- A knack for putting things in a bigger context: a universal context of meaning
- Connecting to the collective unconscious

CHAPTER 8

EXTRAVERTED THINKING (Te)

In this chapter, we seek to present a picture of the "pure" Extraverted Thinking that we would see if we could carefully remove it from its natural state where it is influenced and colored by all the other elements of personality. Though no process actually exists separated from the rest of the personality, the portrait that follows reflects core characteristics that are in play whenever Extraverted Thinking is engaged at a conscious level.

Dominant for ESTJ and ENTJ

Auxiliary for ISTJ and INTJ

Extraverted Thinking most clearly resembles the descriptions in the following pages when it is in the dominant (first) position. In fact, these descriptions are based on input from people for whom the process is dominant (ESTJ and ENTJ). But even with Extraverted Thinking in the first position, what you observe will vary noticeably depending on other factors—particularly whether it is paired up with Introverted Sensing or Introverted Intuiting in the auxiliary (second) position.

In order to draw a complete picture of the "essence" of Extraverted Thinking, one must use bits and pieces that cannot individually demonstrate "pure" Te. Like the splashes of color in an impressionist painting, however, the bullets in this chapter, when taken all together, reveal a vivid portrait that will enable you to recognize Extraverted Thinking when you see it. Knowing what the process would look like if it could be separated from other influences is the foundation of process watching, the practice that will quickly take you as far as you want to go in understanding personality.

Extraverted Thinking is a decision-making process. It focuses on the objective, external world by instituting systems of organization and assigning all information to a place within an appropriate system, based upon quantifiable comparison. Te wants to evaluate, decide, and complete a task using a system of logical binary judgments.

KEY FEATURES

Extraverted Thinking

- Adopts or develops applicable standards to guide decisions.
- Is driven to structure and organize the external world.
- Sorts everything in the world to its proper place in an organized system.
- Applies objective logic within a framework of policies, standard procedures, operational guidelines, or some other common system of guiding rules.
- Views creating and maintaining systems that take care of people as more effective and therefore more important than taking care of individuals directly.
- Is energized by reaching goals or achieving an end result.
- Seeks clarity and order in the environment.

WHAT'S GOING ON?

Extraverted Thinking

- Looks for logical organization or structure in the tangible, external world.
- Employs proven analytical tools.
- Assembles the rules of organization to function like a matrix.
- Can spot illogic and inconsistencies immediately.
- Is analytical.
- Is exemplified by the western scientific process of painstakingly methodical experimentation that examines one variable at a time.
- Strives for equality in dealing with all things, including people.
- Seeks clarity through order.

When people are using their preferred Extraverted Thinking

- They need to use systems that define how things interact and interrelate, such as the laws of physics, to provide frameworks for logical organization and analysis.
- The structure of the process is visible. It could be recorded, explained, and even repeated, as when a second team of scientists duplicates an experiment to confirm the findings of the first team.

They need a system in which all relationships are known in order for the logic of the decision-making process to operate effectively.

They seek clear standards or systems that are broad in scope because such frameworks can be applied to many different situations.

They are sometimes driven to extremes by their desire to anticipate every possible contingency. They may create ponderous institutionalized systems, such as complex government bureaucracies, as a result.

They are most comfortable working within a mechanistic, cause-and-effect model.

The clarity and specificity that they desire is often found in laws, rules, regulations, policies, procedures, and standards.

Broad standards such as the sweeping declarations of the U.S. Constitution's Bill of Rights and Christianity's golden rule are ideal since they can be used almost universally.[15]

Their approach is to methodically move from the facts, through an orderly process, to an end result.

They want to use clear-cut, tangible criteria that are measurable and quantifiable, such as "more" or "bigger," as opposed to qualitative criteria, such as "better" or "more important."

They use the tactic of reducing every choice to a sequence of yes-or-no decisions. Labeling, quantifying, applying objective standards, and analyzing are all techniques that support this reductionist approach.

Their decision-making process makes use of measurable, quantifiable data that can be evaluated on a binary matrix. This provides the framework for the yes-or-no decisions.

They pursue equality through consistent application of the rules. A need to make exceptions to the rules indicates a need to improve the rules. A perfect world would have perfect rules so that exceptions would never need to be made.

Though end results may be their conscious focus, the act of task completion itself is the driving need.

Task completion is their payoff, and the need for a sense of movement toward completion is powerful. Setbacks or a sense of stagnation can be very frustrating.

- If they cannot attain the closure of completing a task, measurable progress is reassuring.
- A series of short-term, intermediate goals or milestones can be very helpful as a way of showing that progress is, indeed, being made.
- If they have no sense of progress being made or they feel that a task is behind schedule, this may lead to high levels of frustration, even anxiety or panic.
- They tend to focus on the task at hand, not on the broader ramifications. They may, for example, neglect to consider the impact on the work team when they are choosing the team's most efficient path to a goal.
- They often need to verbalize the process—to think out loud.

FROM THE OUTSIDE, LOOKING IN

When we experience people who are engaging their preferred Extraverted Thinking, they

- Endeavor to ensure that everything and everyone is treated equally by following policies and procedures.
- Seem to maintain a standard of equality that guides their treatment of people.
- Thrive in a hierarchy where relationships are guided by clear rules, such as the military, the Catholic Church, or a traditional corporate structure.
- Want to know what the goal or desired outcome is before they begin a task.
- Can be relied upon to have a contingency plan.
- Are often the first to produce results when assigned a task. The results are almost always quantifiable.
- Produce the criteria that are needed for a team to make decisions.
- Often use a checklist to make sure tasks are accomplished.
- Need to physically organize their personal space and sometimes try to organize the space of others.
- Need to talk out the logic and underlying assumptions of decisions.
- Do not often say "I think"; it goes without saying. Almost everything you hear from them is thinking verbalized.
- May be perceived as cold since what you hear is their objective, impersonal logic.

- Often imply "you should" or "they ought to" when they express an opinion.
- Often sound more rigid than they are. Thinking out loud sounds a lot like stating decisions. In actuality, as long as they are still talking, they probably have not yet reached a final decision.
- May preface everything they say with an overview of what they are going to say, such as "We need to cut costs. Here is a rough outline of how we can do it."
- Usually try to determine whether someone is competent and whether his or her information is credible and objective before listening to what that person has to say.
- Often start with a distinct agenda, then reference the applicable rules, then go through a series of mini-decisions that will lead to the ultimate decision: Which result is more desirable? Which action will produce that result? What staffing will be required to support that action?
- Can appear harsh and judgmental to people around them. Thinking is critical by definition.
- Take care of people in a broad, systemic way. They gravitate, for example, toward trying to fix the healthcare system rather than focusing on taking care of individuals' health problems.
- Have a defensible position for every question or issue.
- Have a logical rationale for their every action.
- Tend to be decisive. Decisions are usually either "thumbs-up" or "thumbs-down" with no gray area.
- Strive for closure. They are uncomfortable moving on to another task before completing the one they are doing.
- Can sometimes take the drive to reach closure through dispassionate logic to its extreme. It can become a mind-set wherein the end seems to justify the means.
- Seem prone to becoming staunch defenders and enforcers of the prevailing laws and rules. They are often involved in creating the laws or rules.
- Are very systematic and structured.

CONTRIBUTIONS
Special perspectives and approaches of Extraverted Thinking

- The Newtonian view of a universe that consists of objects that act upon each other in predictable, quantifiable ways
- Laws, rules, regulations, and standard operating procedures
- Logical, standardized filing systems
- Outlines
- Prioritization
- Providing logical structure to enable organizations to attain their desired end result
- Giving others a starting place for their work or discussion by presenting a specific position
- Equality

FROM THE INSIDE
Paraphrased descriptions of what it is like to make decisions through one's preferred Extraverted Thinking

- I enjoy crossing items off "to-do" lists. If a completed task is not on my list, I may put it on the list and then cross it off to give myself a sense of accomplishment.
- No matter what it is, I need to analyze or organize it.
- I need to talk in order to think.
- When someone asks me a question, I often just start talking it out. I may not know the answer until I hear myself say it.
- I like respectful, nonpersonal debate because that's how I think.
- I'm very much in the habit of speaking in order to clarify my thoughts.
- I hate it when people at work try to stop a good debate, mistaking it for an argument. Discussion gives me new ideas and allows me to work them through with others.
- I can carry an analysis of something to only a certain level in my own head. To go any deeper, I need someone to be my sounding board. If I can't do that, then writing it down, diagramming, outlining, or even talking aloud to myself is helpful.

I view competence as being extremely important. I strive for competence in all that I do.

It's frustrating when I can see the logical order of things and others refuse to see it or discuss it.

The ideas of weighted data and of sliding scales conflict with my need for an even-handed application of the standards and rules.

My fondness for debate makes some see me as angry or confrontational.

I believe there is always an order, law, rule, or regulation to be followed, though sometimes it may not be obvious to others.

I highly value competence in others and in myself. It's something I always look for. I am really attracted to competent, results-oriented people.

I may not know a lot about a topic, but I have an opinion. I'll know more about what it is after I start talking.

I know that I can come across as being cold and impersonal.

I say, "Be prepared!" I always have a contingency plan. In fact, I have contingency plans for my contingency plans.

I always arrive at meetings prepared, with an agenda, and on time.

Picture several file cabinets, each labeled according to a system. Each file cabinet has labeled drawers, which contain clearly labeled dividers, which in turn hold clearly labeled folders. I organize by means of an external system, one that others can quickly and clearly understand.

I automatically prepare outlines for everything. It is my way of structuring a problem so I know how to tackle it. In school I started all my papers by making an outline, whether it was required or not.

Creating and improving structure in my job is exciting.

Everything can be reduced to cause and effect.

I have the entire year planned in advance.

If I don't know exactly how and when I'm going to accomplish tasks, I get worried that I won't be able to get everything done.

There's a place for everything and everything has its place.

I have a lot of difficulty with the concept of paradox. The idea that two seemingly contradictory explanations can both be true blows my mind. It has to be either one or the other.

- I need to "discuss" my ideas with my partner. Even if I'm not really listening to what he says, I need him as a sounding board. I am really mostly listening to myself to find out what I think.
- I need external structure. I'm sure that's why I made a career in the military.
- I enjoy balancing my checkbook and organizing my possessions and spaces.
- I organize and orchestrate everything. Even my vacations are planned down to the last detail. My family insists that there has to be some spontaneity, so I put times for that in the schedule too.
- I enjoy planning vacations. I enjoy the planning more than the actual vacation. When we drive, I always have several backup plans: a best route, a best alternate route, and so on.
- In my garage, I've traced the outline of each tool on the wall in the place where it belongs so there can be no mistake about what goes where.
- When I proofread this manuscript, I knew immediately when a sentence was not structured correctly.

VIGNETTES

Scenes from the world of Extraverted Thinking

- In a "type-alike" group exercise, our group had to identify the priorities first. What is most important? What's less important? Half of our time was used in creating structure in this way and in identifying the desired end result. After that, we could quickly proceed with accomplishing the task itself.
- Intending to say that she "thinks by talking," a workshop participant instead stated that she "talks by thinking." It was an understandable slip. To her, talking and thinking are essentially synonymous.
- In task-focused workshop exercises, the members of this type-alike group almost always map out how they will approach the task before doing anything else. They either create a timeline or they outline the steps to follow to reach the goal.
- In a workshop exercise, this type-alike group found it extremely uncomfortable to be asked to determine criteria to use in making

a decision, when the information provided was not sufficient for creating good criteria. The lack of data, combined with the drive to complete the task, created a situation that was very stressful.

GIFTS

Unique strengths of Extraverted Thinking

Organizing ideas, objects, information, and so on in the external world to help others understand and use them

Summarizing and codify a nation's or culture's shared vision and morality into laws

Leading logical group decision making

Decisiveness

Contingency planning

Reliability in completing a task

Equal treatment of all

Objectivity

CHAPTER 9

INTROVERTED THINKING (Ti)

In this chapter, we seek to present a picture of the "pure" Introverted Thinking that we would see if we could carefully remove it from its natural state where it is influenced and colored by all the other elements of personality. Though no process actually exists separated from the rest of the personality, the portrait that follows reflects core characteristics that are in play whenever Introverted Thinking is engaged at a conscious level.

**Dominant for
ISTP and INTP**

**Auxiliary for
ESTP and ENTP**

Introverted Thinking most clearly resembles the descriptions in the following pages when it is in the dominant (first) position. In fact, these descriptions are based on input from people for whom the process is dominant (ISTP and INTP). But even with Introverted Thinking in the first position, what you observe will vary noticeably depending on other factors—particularly whether it is paired up with Extraverted Sensing or Extraverted Intuiting in the auxiliary (second) position.

In order to draw a complete picture of the "essence" of Introverted Thinking, one must use bits and pieces that cannot individually demonstrate "pure" Ti. Like the splashes of color in an impressionist painting, however, the bullets in this chapter, when taken all together, reveal a vivid portrait that will enable you to recognize Introverted Thinking when you see it. Knowing what the process would look like if it could be separated from other influences is the foundation of process watching, the practice that will quickly take you as far as you want to go in understanding personality.

Introverted Thinking is a decision-making process. It focuses on the subjective, internal world of underlying principles and truths by creating original systems and categories and assigning all information to a place within the appropriate framework, based upon logical analysis. Ti wants to attain internal precision through logical evaluation and decision making.

KEY FEATURES

Introverted Thinking

- Has an inner focus on logical analysis.
- Wants to make decisions based on an inner framework of principles and truths.
- Creates a precise and refined gridlike system of categorization for sorting information in order to make decisions.
- Builds a subjective internal framework to structure and guide its analysis.
- Focuses upon how tasks get accomplished.
- Seeks internal precision.
- Is driven to understand systems in terms of logical relationships: if A, then B.

WHAT'S GOING ON?

Introverted Thinking

- Builds a logical framework that contains precise categories.
- Uses categories that are created by and are unique to the individual.
- Uses principles that contain logical relationships. Unlike values, they can be debated and defended logically and revised as necessary.
- Depends upon principles as the foundation for analytical decision making in the same way that beliefs are the foundation for values-based decision making.
- Employs systems and categories to attain internal order and precision.
- Lends itself well to understanding work processes.

When people are using their preferred Introverted Thinking

- They trust and rely upon their unique framework of internally synthesized concepts, principles, and knowledge.
- Expanding upon basic principles guides them in creating their original classification systems and categories.
- They work within a framework that is created and used internally.
- Precise internal categories are used to classify information from the environment in order to deal with current or future external events.

- They use external ideas in unique, subjective ways. The ideas found in the environment are rarely adopted in their original form. They are more often used as raw material for designing and building unique internal systems.
- They will revise an internal framework to integrate new information. For example, they may have to deal with a new computer system that works very differently from their old one. It may not fit with their existing internal logic. In this case, their entire internal framework must be recreated to incorporate the new information and new procedures.
- Determining the place of everything in the system and its position in relation to everything else is how they make sense of the world.
- They find creating, refining, and re-refining organizing systems to be an energizing outlet for their creativity and originality.
- They usually focus on the process of group interaction more than on the group's goal.
- If new information does not fit within the existing system of classification, they must create a new category for it. Sometimes the entire framework must be reconstructed.
- They use a cyclical, zeroing-in thought process. They go through successive cycles of thinking about something, with the thinking becoming more and more refined with each cycle.
- They must categorize people, objects, and events in order to identify them. Categorization involves identifying properties and characteristics of a person, object, or event, and then sorting through ever-more precise categories until a place in the system is found where only that one item fits.
- Their logic is objective, but the framework within which it works is very subjective. Thus, their decision-making process is one of subjective logic.
- They relate to people through guiding principles like fairness and truth.
- They want to know exactly how everything works.

FROM THE OUTSIDE, LOOKING IN

When we experience people who are engaging their preferred Introverted Thinking, they

- Can sometimes be very slow in coming to a decision. If no appropriate internal category exists to accommodate new information or events, they need to first revise, or sometimes reinvent, the entire internal framework before making the decision.
- Sometimes seem as if they are devaluing people, but they are not actually making a value judgment at all.
- Can become confused when their internal thought process does not match what is going on in the external world.
- May show tension and frustration with people who have reached conclusions that are different from their own. This is not unusual because their internal thinking process is unique and usually not shared with or understood by others.
- Will defend their principles over all else.
- May sound unemotional and uninterested when discussing anything that does not fit into their internal framework.
- Show their passion when attempting to explain their original thoughts. They may even display a sense of urgency if others are not being patient with their detailed explanation.
- Tend to say either too much or too little. Often their level and style of communication is determined primarily by how much time they have spent carefully working out the details.
- Tend to say "I think." They are aware of their personal thought process and want others to appreciate that a lot of careful analysis lies behind their conclusions.
- Will often simply state their decision or lay out their conclusion without any explanation. The expectation seems to be that the precision of the logic that brought them to that conclusion will be obvious and unchallengeable.
- May need someone to prompt them to explain how they reached their conclusion or decision.
- Stubbornly resist changing their position.
- Tend to say "my," not "our," when explaining the process or results of a decision-making task. Even if it was a group process, for them it was personal and internal.

- Tend to use carefully formulated, precise language.
- Seek precision from others.
- Frequently rephrase statements back to a speaker in order to refine their understanding. Others may misinterpret this as trying to outdo the speaker or as showing off their intelligence. In fact, they are just trying to make sure that they understand precisely what was said.
- Treat other people's opinions respectfully though certain that their own are correct. Everyone has a right to an opinion.
- May have already made a decision but not tell anyone.
- May ask a lot of questions to try to understand someone else's decision.
- Are usually not very interested in attempts to persuade them, nor are they threatened by the attempts.
- Seem to compete with themselves. They usually reanalyze their decisions, for example, to see how they can be improved.
- May overlook the importance of their relationships with other people. This is especially true if the relationship does not fit into any category in their framework.
- Are hesitant to explain their thinking. Going through their thoughts aloud must be done with precision, so it can be tedious and may be doomed to fail if they are not given the opportunity to fully explain their analysis.
- Often are not aware that their framework for decision making is not universally shared.
- Usually assume that their conclusion or decision is right since they have been so thorough and precise in their logic.
- Are prone to get impatient with people they see as not thinking through the consequences of their own actions.
- Can be confusing to others since they can play the devil's advocate so well. They can switch sides in midsentence and defend another position, causing other people to think that they cannot make up their minds.
- Are generally seen by others as being very intelligent.
- Tend to hide stress. They often show a poker face to others, and people are not sure what is really going on with them.
- Usually their main interests are intellectual and may not be very helpful in social situations. This is likely to be particularly true early in life, when Introverted Thinking is the focus of their type development.
- Are not usually outwardly emotional.

CONTRIBUTIONS

Special perspectives and approaches of Introverted Thinking

- Binomial classification (the system under which all living organisms are named based on categories defined by the shared characteristics of the organisms in that category, and each category is further divided into increasingly specific subcategories)
- A knack for playing the devil's advocate
- Incorporating all the logically connected data into decisions
- Precise logic
- Unified theories, such as relativity, the big bang, and quantum theory
- Finding new ways to analyze or organize
- "Fairness" as a guiding principle
- "Truth" as a guiding principle

FROM THE INSIDE

Paraphrased descriptions of what it is like to make decisions through one's preferred Introverted Thinking

- As a teacher, it is hard for me to facilitate group interactions because I want to get into the discussions and debates.
- It's difficult admitting when I'm wrong because I have invested a lot of time and energy into making a decision. I have really thought it out carefully.
- I always want to know how to do things and to know how things work.
- I have been called "stubborn as a mule" when others have tried to force me to think differently.
- My mind is like a grid with labels at all the grid coordinates. If you looked through a magnifying glass, you might see that each of those intersections is actually made up of a finer grid, which in turn is made up of finer ones, and so on, with correspondingly ever-more refined and more precise category labels.
- I have a mental picture of myself always sifting through dirt with a screen to separate the worthless particles. I'm trying to figure out what is important and where to pile it for later use. Under stress, I seem to

increase the sifting aspect of my activities and find myself unable to make decisions about what to do with the data I collect.

All my life I have thought that I might have some kind of learning disability. Almost everything in school seemed to come much slower to me than it came to others. Elementary school, in particular, rewards the kids who raise their hands or call out the answers first. Now I realize that I just needed time to let my internal logic do its thing.

The answer was clear to me but hard to explain with the precision that it had in my mind.

I like to work alone and figure things out in my own way. Don't try to micromanage me.

Laws are important, but I'm selective about which ones I respect or will follow.

I can easily debate an issue from any position.

I need my job to allow for flexible scheduling and to let me be creative and independent.

I'm a control freak toward myself.

Thinking about something is like using a series of filters; each filter sorts information into a more refined category until I find the unique subcategory where only that one piece belongs.

Once a framework has been constructed, I can deal quickly and easily with new information as long as the new information can be placed in the proper context within the framework.

I feel tremendous satisfaction in being able to make order in my mind from chaotic data.

I'm very independent. It's hard for me to compromise in order to reach a consensus with others. I would much rather continue to disagree than be forced to agree.

My independent logic often leads me to conclusions that could be very unpopular. I rarely say them aloud to anyone except my most trusted friends.

Though I'm not a combative person, if I verbalize my thinking, people often think I'm attacking them because it's usually so contradictory to theirs.

In "type-alike" group exercises, our group usually does a lot of thinking before we start recording anything on the flip chart.

VIGNETTES

Scenes from the world of Introverted Thinking

- In reporting after an exercise, the individual members of this "type-alike" group usually elaborate on what was written on the flip chart. They want to ensure that their own unique perspective is understood. They do not feel a need to come to consensus about what is presented on the flip chart; just to ensure that all the different ideas are presented.

- My wife gets upset with me because of my need to categorize before I act. We live in a rural area that has a lot of bugs. When she sees a bug on the wall or ceiling, she tells me to get up and kill it. I first need to determine how it got inside, what kind of bug it is, how to kill it, whether it will make a mess on the wall, and how I will dispose of it. She expects me to immediately react, but I can't until I have completed my analysis.

- A man who had always questioned his abilities as a writer finally learned that his internal, very precise style of writing just takes longer and uses a different process than the approach he was taught in college. Once he decided to just do it his own way, he turned out to be a very competent writer.

- In an exercise in group decision making, the time constraints were very challenging for our "type-alike" group. The short time frame did not allow for our internal logic process and the group interaction that was required. Anticipating this, we chose to give up on the task and turned the assignment into a game in which we advocated several different positions.

- The search for precision can lead to confusion for others. In a workshop, a participant provided the phase "maximize the takeaway" as his conclusion at the end of an exercise. He had worked long and hard in his mind to come up with this perfect expression of the thought, but no one else knew what he meant. In fact, some participants thought he was trying to show off his intelligence by phrasing his conclusion in a way that they could not understand. The more precisely crafted the wording, the better it may express a unique idea that will not be completely understood by anyone else. It may need to be "translated" into more general, shared terminology for others to understand.

GIFTS

Unique strengths of Introverted Thinking

- Seeing the underlying framework of assumptions and the logical consequences
- Evaluation and planning of organizational process flow
- A knack for thinking outside the box: unconventional perspectives and insights
- Detecting the illogic in conventional wisdom and the dysfunction in commonly accepted behavior
- A capacity for presenting new explanations or conclusions without ego involvement
- Cutting through denial
- The reassuring aura of stability that comes from always having a principle anchoring decisions and actions
- Systems thinking

CHAPTER 10

EXTRAVERTED FEELING (Fe)

In this chapter, we seek to present a picture of the "pure" Extraverted Feeling that we would see if we could carefully remove it from its natural state where it is influenced and colored by all the other elements of personality. Though no process actually exists separated from the rest of the personality, the portrait that follows reflects core characteristics that are in play whenever Extraverted Feeling is engaged at a conscious level.

Extraverted Feeling most clearly resembles the descriptions in the following pages when it is in the dominant (first) position. In fact, these descriptions are based on input from people for whom the process is dominant (ESFJ and ENFJ). But even with Extraverted Feeling in the first position, what you observe will vary noticeably depending on other factors—particularly whether it is paired up with Introverted Sensing or Introverted Intuiting in the auxiliary (second) position.

In order to draw a complete picture of the "essence" of Extraverted Feeling, one must use bits and pieces that cannot individually demonstrate "pure" Fe. Like the splashes of color in an impressionist painting, however, the bullets in this chapter, when taken all together, reveal a vivid portrait that will enable you to recognize Extraverted Feeling when you see it. Knowing what the process would look like if it could be separated from other influences is the foundation of process watching, the practice that will quickly take you as far as you want to go in understanding personality.

Extraverted Feeling is a decision-making process. It focuses on the objective, external world through using cultural value systems and assigning all things to a place within an appropriate system, based on qualitative value. Fe wants to make choices and initiate actions that create and maintain harmony in the outer world.

**Dominant for
ESFJ and ENFJ**

**Auxiliary for
ISFJ and INFJ**

KEY FEATURES

Extraverted Feeling

- Is an objective decision-making process that seeks to create or maintain harmony in the environment.
- Has an outward focus that is primarily about people and their relationships.
- Views people, events, situations, and objects in terms of their effects on people.
- Is actively concerned for others' needs, desires, and values.
- Prefers to avoid outward conflict but can become unyielding in situations involving a threat to another person.
- Establishes and maintains social conventions.
- Is driven to interact with people.

WHAT'S GOING ON?

Extraverted Feeling

- Takes cultural and societal values and norms as the starting point for decision-making.
- Seeks to understand what is important to others.
- Wants to understand people's needs, desires, and values in terms of how they support and align with the values of society and subcultures, such as organizations.
- Seeks to help maintain external harmony.
- Focuses on interpersonal harmony and relationships.
- Is values based, not logic based. Though rational and objective, the process is not logical; it is evaluative.
- Seeks external harmony, even if it comes at the cost of creating internal conflict.

When people are using their preferred Extraverted Feeling

- Social value is their top priority.
- They tend to focus on society and groups more than on specific individuals.

The value or worth of something guides their actions. For example, they will probably obey speed limits in order to avoid hurting anyone rather than because they might get caught and fined.

They have a keen awareness of the impact of decisions on others.

They are strong presences in any room. Everyone is aware of them.

Their values guide their actions through "shoulds" and "should nots."

They seek to have a positive impact on people and to avoid hurting anyone.

They want to nurture people, whether or not the people want or need to be nurtured.

When making decisions, they usually move very quickly to closure.

They often defend people and express their values by taking up causes.

All of their decisions take into account the impact on people.

They tend to overlook their own emotional and physical needs.

They need to discuss their thoughts and concerns about people with others.

They want to take care of everyone physically, emotionally, and spiritually.

They often have a very hard time focusing on taking care of themselves. It is common for their own physical needs to be neglected until a personal health crisis demands their attention.

Ensuring that people feel valued is a high priority.

They maintain the standards for societal values and behavior.

FROM THE OUTSIDE, LOOKING IN

When we experience people who are engaging their preferred Extraverted Feeling, they

Seem to know the appropriate thing to say or do in every situation. They attend weddings and funerals, for example, to show that they care.

Focus on their relationships with people.

Tend to take care of people's needs collectively more often than individually.

- Maintain the cultural norms of a society, a country, a business organization, and civic and religious groups.
- Act as the keepers of social conventions, etiquette, politeness, and acceptable behavior.
- Tend to remember and celebrate all special occasions, such as birthdays and anniversaries. They are the ones in an organization who usually get the cakes, flowers, and cards for others.
- Usually put others ahead of themselves.
- Seem determined to help people whether they want to be helped or not.
- May go to extreme lengths to provide what they deem is needed to maintain external harmony. This can sometimes come at a great personal cost. They often adapt their style and behavior to the group they are with.
- Personalize others' discomfort or pain. They seem driven to keep others from being embarrassed or hurt.
- Observe the little niceties that lubricate social interaction. Saying "please" and "thank you," for example, helps to keep relationships harmonious.
- Don't usually say "I feel." Their language tends to be inclusive rather than personal. For example, they will use the word "we" a lot.
- Give praise freely and expect them to be returned.
- Say or imply "should" a lot in an attempt to enforce social rules.
- Do what is expected or appropriate for a situation. They may praise something, for example, because doing so is the socially correct reaction.
- Can come across as being insincere or too nice.
- Work to ensure that everyone is included, heard, and shown respect. They often ask, "What do you think?" or "Are you okay with that?"
- Empathize with others and say so.
- Often express the emotional content for a group.
- View conversation as a form of action. You may hear them use phrases such as "let's talk it over," "we can work it out," and "two heads are better than one."
- Listen empathetically to people's concerns, issues, and stories. They always respond to let people know they have been heard.

- Always seem to know the right words to say. They are natural greeting-card writers.
- Value harmonious working relationships.
- View warmth and fellowship as extremely important.
- Take conflict and indifference personally.
- Will go to great lengths to give and receive validation.
- May suddenly realize that they are not being taken care of. They may feel martyred and become angry with those whom they see as shirking that obligation.
- Are usually the ones who feel responsible for bringing up issues that threaten the family, like the need to balance family priorities with the demands of work.
- Are available and present for others.
- Can brighten up a room by their presence.
- Work actively and tirelessly to maintain harmony in their environment.
- May become a crusader for social causes.
- Are usually perceived as cheerful and caring and good conversationalists.
- Tend to be the perfect hosts and hostesses.
- Organize their home and work space to promote the comfort of their guests. They have enough comfortable chairs for everyone, a pleasant color scheme, plants and artwork that add to the atmosphere, and plenty of good food and drink.

CONTRIBUTIONS

Special perspectives and approaches of Extraverted Feeling

- Appreciative inquiry
- A facility for creating employee events and programs, such as the company picnic, the company Christmas party, employee-assistance programs, and opportunities for career development and continuing education
- Awareness and promotion of appropriate behavior
- Awareness and consideration of the impact of decisions on people

- A capacity for helping others physically, emotionally, and spiritually
- Consensus building
- Political correctness
- Civility

FROM THE INSIDE

Paraphrased descriptions of what it is like to make decisions through one's preferred Extraverted Feeling:

- My values shape how I live. They come with a thousand "shoulds" and "should nots."
- I am always aware of what behavior is acceptable and what is not.
- It's hard for me to be isolated from people.
- I like good vibes. I try to fix conflict. I am uneasy when people start to disagree and there is tension between them.
- Like the stereotypical bartender, I am a good listener and adviser.
- I sometimes take on and verbalize the unspoken feelings of the room without even knowing it.
- I can get so enthralled by someone else's story that I lose myself in it.
- I just know what everyone needs. I assume, too often, that others know this too.
- Even when I was a little girl, I would always make my own greeting cards and write a special verse that was perfect for a particular person.
- People need people.
- It's very important to me that I feel appreciated.
- I respond strongly to both positive strokes and negative criticism.
- I often find it difficult to give feedback that is critical because I am concerned about how it will impact the person I am talking to.
- If someone is displeased with me, it bothers me so much that I can't hear what that person is saying.
- I just know about people. I know about what they need and want. I always find the perfect gift for everyone.
- How we work together is as important as what we accomplish.
- I really don't like making decisions alone. I need to talk them out with others. The greater the impact of a decision on people, the more I need to discuss it.

- If I'm alone, I often talk to myself out loud to keep myself company.
- I have always had difficulty understanding what is meant by the phrase "objective criteria." Criteria are about people, and there is no way to be objective about people.
- I have to be doing something that lets me feel that I'm helping other people. I have to feel needed.
- My husband always tells me, "Why don't you stop taking care of others for a while and take care of yourself?" or "Let someone take care of you for a change."
- I like movies with interesting relationships.
- I've always focused on what I know others want me to do.
- I feel compelled to take on the emotional burdens of the world.
- I have a very hard time saying no. It's difficult not to volunteer, even when I'm not asked. One of the biggest challenges of my life is accepting that I can't do it all, that I can't take care of everybody.
- I'm not good at helping others sort out their own wants and needs. I often get impatient because I already know what is best for them.
- I know that I sometimes micromanage relationships and take away people's opportunity to work problems out for themselves.
- I think I often experience other people's emotions more intensely than they do.
- I tend to cry at movies and even feel embarrassed for the characters.
- First, I have to get to know you better. That's what is most important.
- Knowing what gifts to give people is very easy for me. I always assume that everyone knows what I want too. I'm afraid that I often make the same assumption about other things too: that everyone will always know and provide what I want and need if they care about me.
- I can easily get lost in arranging the details of social events like seating, flower arrangements, and food presentation. I want everything to be just right for the guests.

VIGNETTES

Scenes from the world of Extraverted Feeling

- In "type-alike" group activities, our team spends a lot of time at the beginning of the exercise getting to know each other. We first need to make sure that there is harmony in the group. We need to establish a sense of who everyone is in order to operate as a team. During the exercise, we all make an effort to ensure that everyone's idea is heard and captured. The results of our work are usually reached by consensus.

- Last year, I hit the campaign trail for my daughter, who was running for public office. I found that I was really good at door-to-door campaigning. I could initiate that kind of light, friendly, content-free conversation all day long.

- A teacher had two days scheduled at school to catch up on paperwork while the students were on vacation. It was very difficult, however, for him to sit, read, and correct papers with no interaction. He found himself getting up and visiting other teachers. He noted that "the interaction is where I get my energy."

- When giving a dinner party, I need to prearrange everything. I don't want to be cooking during the party. I want everything to be perfect. I need to have everything done by the time the first guest arrives because I know that from then on, I won't be able to concentrate on anything but the people. Once they start arriving, I'm totally focused on making sure they are comfortable and enjoying themselves. If they weren't, that would be horrible!

- If I think there's a problem affecting the people closest to me, I just have to do something about it. When my daughter was having problems with her guidance counselor at school, I went to the school and confronted the counselor. My daughter didn't want me to go, but I really didn't have a choice. I just had to do whatever it took to take care of her.

GIFTS

Unique strengths of Extraverted Feeling

- A talent for taking care of the needs of others

- Maintaining the social structure, standards, and conventions of a culture
- Maintaining society's moral codes
- Empathy
- A knack for appreciating and valuing others for who they are and the gifts that they possess
- Personal warmth
- Compassion
- Serving as the world's social conscience

CHAPTER 11

INTROVERTED FEELING (Fi) - Meaning

In this chapter, we seek to present a picture of the "pure" Introverted Feeling that we would see if we could carefully remove it from its natural state where it is influenced and colored by all the other elements of personality. Though no process actually exists separated from the rest of the personality, the portrait that follows reflects core characteristics that are in play whenever Introverted Feeling is engaged at a conscious level.

Introverted Feeling most clearly resembles the descriptions in the following pages when it is in the dominant (first) position. In fact, these descriptions are based on input from people for whom the process is dominant (ISFP and INFP). But even with Introverted Feeling in the first position, what you observe will vary noticeably depending on other factors—particularly whether it is paired up with Extraverted Sensing or Extraverted Intuiting in the auxiliary (second) position.

In order to draw a complete picture of the "essence" of Introverted Feeling, one must use bits and pieces that cannot individually demonstrate "pure" Fi. Like the splashes of color in an impressionist painting, however, the bullets in this chapter, when taken all together, reveal a vivid portrait that will enable you to recognize Introverted Feeling when you see it. Knowing what the process would look like if it could be separated from other influences is the foundation of process watching, the practice that will quickly take you as far as you want to go in understanding personality.

Introverted Feeling is a decision-making process. It focuses on the subjective, internal world of absolute personal value systems and assesses all things based upon whether they uphold the values, conflict with them, or have no impact. Fi wants to make choices and act in ways that create and maintain inner harmony.

**Dominant for
ISFP and INFP**

**Auxiliary for
ESFP and ENFP**

KEY FEATURES

Introverted Feeling

- Is a subjective decision-making process that is based on personal values.
- Holds private and nonnegotiable core values deep within.
- Accepts life as it happens and embraces the individuality of others, up to a point.
- Quietly exudes a peaceful, grounded aura.
- Does not tolerate violations of its core beliefs.
- Relates to people one-on-one through a fine-tuned sensitivity to the inner life of others.
- Seeks inner harmony.

WHAT'S GOING ON?

Introverted Feeling

- Is the most subjective of the four decision-making processes.
- Probably originates many concepts that have come to be seen as unchallengeable rights, such as justice and freedom.
- Develops expertise in recognizing and cultivating inner harmony.
- Has a focus on the individual, not the collective.
- Is the only mental process with a truly nonnegotiable element.

When people are using their preferred Introverted Feeling

- Their beliefs are personal and not influenced by the established value systems of their culture.
- They may hold personal, unique versions of widely accepted cultural values. Some of their values may be unrelated to the existing cultural norms, and some may even conflict with them.
- They hold deep, not broad, beliefs.
- Their awareness of a conflict with their values often comes literally through gut feelings. These physical sensations signal when something is wrong or out of line with their internal values and beliefs.
- Sometimes it is only when their values are violated that they become aware of the values.
- They may view virtually anything as innately good or innately bad, as positive or negative.

- They use a decision-making process that is too personal to share. Discussing it is not generally a productive exercise.
- They need to "feel right" about things.
- Nurturing and protecting their inner emotional life is their primary goal.
- Internal harmony is more than desirable: it is critical to their well-being.
- Their aim is an internal life that is Utopian and not defined or limited by the realities of the physical world, such as human nature or the laws of physics.
- Comfort lies within their internal belief systems.
- They have difficulty consciously accessing their values. They may not even be consciously aware of what some of them are.
- They often have great sensitivity to internal harmony or disharmony in others.
- They are adept at knowing when something is wrong or right with others.
- Bringing their inner system of values to fruition in the real world is usually not important to them.

FROM THE OUTSIDE, LOOKING IN

When we experience people who are engaging their preferred Introverted Feeling, they

- Are outwardly very tolerant of other people's values, as long as those values are not in direct conflict with their own.
- Have a strong sense of right and wrong.
- Hold passionately to their internal beliefs.
- Tend to be easygoing, tolerant, and flexible unless their core beliefs become involved.
- May not be able to find the right words to adequately express their values, even when these values do come to the surface.
- Show so little of themselves to the outside world that who they are may remain a mystery to people around them, often even to their spouses.
- Are often not aware of how they affect the world and people around them.
- May take very good care of people one-on-one, based upon recognizing and accepting that we all have unique needs and values.

- Have sensitivity to others' inner calmness or turmoil, which often results in their forming relatively deep personal relationships. They will not force themselves on others, but they will usually know, for example, about the personal lives and issues of their coworkers. They know who is married, who has children issues, who has elder-care issues, who has relationship problems, and who is unhappy in their job; and they will often try to help them out.
- Have an essential honesty and integrity that is not usually displayed for others to see. It is who they are, part of their very being.
- Learn not to talk about hot-button topics, such as religion or politics. Their values are personal and subjective, so they may not match the culturally acceptable or politically correct values of the day. Since their deeply held values cannot be altered, they assume that everyone else's values are unchangeable too, so talking about them can accomplish nothing but to create stress.
- Reveal clues to their real core values through the level of passion in their voice when they speak about something that is important to them.
- Make statements about decisions like "this feels right to me."
- Will listen without challenging or making a judgment right up to the point where something conflicts with their values. At that point, the violator may simply be shut off, instantly excluded from their world.
- May cut off a relationship because their value system has been threatened, without giving any indication that anything has changed. The other person may not even be aware of what has happened.
- Will resist data that appears to conflict with their values. In such a situation, they adapt very slowly or not at all.
- May express their values in "I feel" statements since their need for inner harmony is personal.
- Often form strong bonds with other people who share the Introverted Feeling preference. The bonds can be so strong that there is no great need to talk. Just being together is enough.
- Are usually very easy for others to talk to. They are very nonjudgmental, as long as their private belief system is not violated.
- Assume that everyone's values are absolute, so there is no sense in disputing or even trying to understand them.

- Have unquestioning faith in their own values.
- Usually appear neutral on the outside. Internally they can be warm, caring, and empathetic, or they may be critical and scornful if their values have been threatened. It is usually hard for others to tell what is going on inside.
- Need to be drawn in to a decision-making process when the decision has nothing to do with their values. In such a situation, they will usually not get very energized by the discussion. They may not have a strong opinion one way or another. This is often mistaken for indecisiveness.
- With multiple choices, they may care about some but not all of the options. They may say, for example, "I don't care which restaurant we choose, but definitely not that one because they don't pay their staff a living wage."
- Provide the ethical backbone of any country, culture, ethnic group, or organization.
- Adapt to situations by ignoring anything that is unpleasant or distasteful unless it violates a value. Until a value is violated, nothing brings out their energy or effort to become involved.
- Will usually leave a job, regardless of the consequences, if they find that their values are at odds with those of their employer.
- Tend to be polite people.
- Influence others primarily through their behavior. They lead by example.
- Project an inner harmony and an easygoing attitude, regardless of what is actually going on inside.
- Tend to be very genuine and sincere.
- Exude an inner dignity and charm: the perfect gentleman or lady.
- Often attract others to them because of their serenity.
- May arrange their personal spaces to promote serenity.

CONTRIBUTIONS

Special perspectives and approaches of Introverted Feeling

- Awareness of the human needs and values that are in play for individuals who are involved in group activities

- Working quietly behind the scenes to safeguard other people's beliefs and values
- A talent for providing a reliable barometer of the level of emotional safety in a group
- Serving as the ethical backbone of an organization
- Nonjudgmental tolerance of the values of others
- An aura of inner peace and serenity
- A knack for creating emotionally supportive environments
- An inner sense of knowing about people's authenticity

FROM THE INSIDE

Paraphrased descriptions of what it is like to make decisions through one's preferred Introverted Feeling

- My values come from a gut level. If someone ever got me to talk about them, I would be explaining, not discussing, them. The values come first. They are just there.
- If I had felt really strongly about the issue and felt safe to talk about it, I would have said something.
- It's very hard for me to take a stand publicly. I have to spend time trying it on to see whether it feels right. When I do take a stand, it comes out very passionately and I am not open to debating or discussing the issue.
- As a manager, I hate personnel evaluations. I do not like to be evaluated by my manager, and I do not like to evaluate my subordinates. People are who they are and they do what they do. Normally, I don't feel I have a right or a need to judge them. I don't give out many pats on the back either, because I do not need them and I forget that others do.
- I can feel when people are with me or against me.
- I use humor and sarcasm as a way to keep my values from becoming public. I need to deflect attention from this very personal place. If necessary, I may literally run away rather than reveal my values.
- I could never work for someone who has values that conflict with mine.

- My personal space is very important to me. Please don't invade my physical and emotional space.
- Rules have to feel right to me or I'll ignore them.
- What I need most from people is affirmation, acceptance, and my freedom.
- I hate being labeled or told what I think. If people don't check with me, they do not have a clue who I really am.
- My internal beliefs are very powerful and nonnegotiable. They just are.
- I have a sense of right or wrong and of good or bad, which usually comes to me as a physical sensation in the very center of my body.
- "Gut feeling" is a literal description. When something is wrong, it makes me sick to my stomach.
- If I even try to compromise my values, my heart starts pounding.
- I often know a lot about the details of the lives of individuals in my circle, though very few people, if any, know me as intimately.
- Often, in order to avoid hurting other people, I will do whatever it takes to please them, unless it comes to the point where they are violating my boundaries. Then I'll close the door on them without even being aware that I have shut them out.
- I've learned that I need to let people know about my boundaries sooner. I've learned that they can't see them and may violate them by accident.
- I'm really good at helping in an emotional crisis.
- I pick up a lot on other people's feelings, often before they do themselves.
- I have a sense of right and wrong that I cannot explain. When it comes into play, it cannot be shaken. It's just innate, a part of who I am.
- If someone affronts my values, I will cut him off so quickly that he will just be gone. I will probably never initiate contact with that person again. I will never say anything to hurt him but I will have lost all respect for him as a person.
- I'm an educator of adults. This is my life's work and I approach it with a passion. Even after all these years, I still have problems

when I have to evaluate projects or papers. If the students have given everything they can, it does not feel right for me to assign grades to their work.

I am like a house with many different rooms. The family rooms are hectic, loud, and full of people. However, the rooms where I prefer to spend most of my time are furnished and decorated to promote tranquility and nurture my spirit. They are very private, and only I am allowed to go there.

I don't understand how people can live in conflict with their values.

I could never do something just because someone else wants me to do it if it doesn't feel right to me.

I don't like my sister. But I love her because she's family. Loving my family is an important value to me.

VIGNETTES

Scenes from the world of Introverted Feeling

A woman mentally checked out of an exercise because she knew there would not be enough time for her introverted decision making. She could not do the assignment. Her need to contribute in her own preferred way could not be met while she complied with the group's mandate to complete the task. She felt that her only option was to cut herself off from the exercise in order to resolve the inner conflict.

A woman reported that at work, group decision making often moves too fast. It does not allow time for private consideration. It is helpful if information and an agenda are provided in advance of a meeting to give her an opportunity to reflect. Even then it is usually difficult for her to participate in a way that is comfortable unless the discussion is deferred to a later meeting.

When my son was a teenager, I inadvertently violated a deeply held value of his. He would not talk to me for the next two years.

My husband and younger brother both prefer Introverted Feeling. When they served as pallbearers at our mother's funeral, they wore flannel shirts and blue jeans. They just knew it was the right way for them to honor her. They had been with her every day and had never dressed or behaved like anyone but themselves for her. They were not going to change that for her funeral just to please others. It did not bother them in the least that most of my aunts and uncles, concerned about what is appropriate and customary, were appalled.

GIFTS

Unique strengths of Introverted Feeling

- Knowing when others are in internal distress
- A talent for helping people one-on-one
- A knack for accepting and trusting people
- Exceptional authenticity and sincerity
- Moral stability
- Spirituality
- Gentleness
- Patience

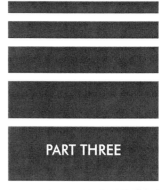

PART THREE

BEYOND
PROCESS WATCHING

CHAPTER 12

THE EIGHT-PROCESS MODEL OF TYPE

The eight-process model is nothing more than a description of theory and practices that have been set forth by C. G. Jung, Katharine Briggs, Isabel Myers, John Beebe, Leona Haas, and others. This view of type is built upon Jung's theory of the psyche (see appendix A), with a specific focus on how the conscious/unconscious aspect influences how we use the eight mental processes. Jung sorted and expanded upon his clinical observations to make broad statements about the workings of the human psyche. Briggs and Myers developed these theories into a framework and tool that made it possible for millions to benefit from their insights. Beebe has helped carry the theory forward to explore the importance of an individual's access to all eight processes, with each process carrying an archetypal "job description" by virtue of its position in the sequence of preference (see appendix B). Haas has now increased the accessibility of the model by describing the processes in detail and developing an innovative, effective methodology for teaching, giving feedback, verifying true type, and providing practical applications of Beebe's theory.

The eight-process model rests upon the understanding that preference is a key aspect of type that affects how we use all eight of the mental processes. Our innate individual preference for one process over others extends in a predictable sequence through all eight. As we scan down our sequence of processes from our most preferred to least preferred, each successive process is innately less comfortable and requires more energy to use. In addition, each one is increasingly difficult to develop and to access. Thus, the further we climb down our ladder of preferences, the more likely it is that the processes located there will remain in the domain of the unconscious: untamed, primitive, and beyond our willful control.

You have to have a respect for the psyche to do this work.
John Beebe

Notice, though, that we always qualify such statements. We say that the processes further down our sequence of preferences are *increasingly difficult* to develop and less likely to naturally become conscious. Although the eight-process model provides a useful guide for understanding how we do or do not develop our mental processes as we mature, this normal progression of type development is not a hard-and-fast rule. As noted before, we are complex beings leading complicated lives. It is very common for school, work, or home life to force us to develop processes in ways that the model does not predict. Many of us develop some of our processes out of sequence. Understanding our preferred sequence, however, can always tell us a lot about the energy required to engage these less accessible processes. No matter how well we develop them, the processes that are not naturally preferred will never be as clear and easy to use as the ones that we do prefer.

Jung wrote that we are born unconscious and that psychological maturing means bringing an increasing number of our unconscious processes further and further into consciousness. This integration of the unconscious into our conscious selves is accomplished through the exploration and use of our less developed processes. Gradually, we become more and more familiar with these neglected parts of ourselves and able to exercise some conscious control over them. This ongoing work of bringing unconscious mental processes gradually into consciousness is known as "individuation." It is how we go about expanding our personal toolkit to include more ways of taking in information and making decisions. The overall picture of personal growth through individuation is known as "type development."

Children normally develop one Perceiving and one Judging process early in life, usually between the ages of six and twenty. Coping with even life's simplest situations requires both taking in information and making decisions and both Extraverting and Introverting, so either the preferred Judging process or the preferred Perceiving process must be Extraverted and the other must be Introverted. Though we can be successful in our early years without having the versatility of adults' broader array of coping strategies, children do need to develop this two-piece toolkit that includes some way of taking in information, a way of making choices, a way of interacting with their environment, and a way of being with themselves.

As we grow, we continue to experiment with different processes to find out what works best for us. Since some of what we need to do can be most successfully accomplished through engaging specific mental processes, gradually normal life experiences drive us to attain some level of familiarity with several of them. This is normal type development.

A recurring situation may force us to use our less preferred processes often enough that they become relatively familiar and conscious. Circumstances such as growing up in a family with an unusually strong and narrow process bias can cause individuals to develop and depend upon processes that are not their innately preferred ones. But Harold Grant has suggested that, barring such strong external influences, the processes are brought into consciousness according to a predictable developmental timetable, as outlined in appendix C.

Type development can, of course, also be pursued intentionally. One of our primary motivations for writing this book is to aid people in pursuing this approach to personal growth. The self-development potential in understanding type has always been one of the primary reasons for people's interest in the subject. We work to develop our mental processes to some degree even if we do not realize that this is what we are doing. We can learn to operate outside the comfort zone of our preferred processes when we become aware of the need to develop specific skills for our job, to cope in school, to adapt to living with someone, or simply to satisfy our innate need to become a more whole person.

The processes that are the most difficult for us to deal with in others are usually the ones that make us uncomfortable from within as well. We may have the same negative reactions to these parts of ourselves as we do externally: dislike, disgust, anger, disrespect, dismissal, and avoidance. In fact, we often refuse to acknowledge that they exist within us at all. By failing to accept this shadow part of ourselves, we set the stage for just about every form of interpersonal conflict that we experience in our lives. Miscommunication, false assumptions, and projection are just a few of the seeds of friction and conflict that have their origins in the limitations of our own type development. But the unconscious processes actually hold a wealth of explanations and answers for us. They hold within them alternative perspectives and ways of operating that can balance the innate bias of our preferred approaches. With an expanded knowledge of type as our guide, our path to greater understanding and acceptance of ourselves becomes much clearer. Self-acceptance is not just about accepting the parts of us that we like or even recognize. Exploring our unconscious shadow side can lead to tremendous personal growth and improvements in virtually every aspect of our lives.

By recognizing our undeveloped, unconscious processes and learning how they fit into our type development, we can begin to understand which of them are not easily accessible for us. We can appreciate the benefits they offer. We can see that these unconscious processes, rather than being places to avoid, are actually opportunities for growth that are waiting for our conscious exploration. It may well be that genius is primarily a matter of an unusually high level of type development, of unconscious potential turned into conscious strengths.

CHAPTER 13

IMPORTANT FACETS AND FACTORS IN EIGHT-PROCESS TYPE

We have stated that the importance of the eight-process model lies in its emphasis on certain aspects of Jung's theory of personality type. Indeed, the model itself is simply a description of what is revealed when we understand the importance of these "facets and factors" and how they mesh together.

THE CAST OF CHARACTERS

Once you become reasonably skilled at recognizing the pure processes, the next step is to begin to look at how they interact. It is accurate to say that we engage the processes one at a time. But it is also true that the processes supporting the one in use are an integral part of the overall picture as well. The interactions of the processes and the dynamics of the system are always a big part of what is going on. What we see is actually a performance by a diverse cast of characters.

The uniqueness of our personal drama is much more than the result of a few stars advancing a simple plot. Secondary and tertiary players, sometimes behind the scenes and sometimes at center stage, are interacting as well, creating layer upon layer of subplots and counter-themes.

In appendix E, you will find our circle of eight-process type, a chart outlining the alignment of the processes in each of the sixteen types. We have also provided, for comparison, a more traditional table of the types, with thumbnail sketches that emphasize the dominant and auxiliary processes (appendix D).

Type differences are more complex than the characteristics associated with each preference. The interaction among preferences is the key to understanding type at a deeper level . . . . The dynamic nature of the human personality and the developmental model underlying psychological type are the elements that keep types from being static boxes into which individuals are fitted. These dynamic elements are why looking at the world through the lens of type can be rewarding —even after fifty years.
    Katherine Myers
    and Linda Kirby

BALANCE

Balance is a key factor in determining which processes team up in a given situation. Not much can happen until Perceiving is complemented with Judging and Extraverting with Introverting or vice versa. As Isabel Myers put it, "The need for such supplementing is obvious. Perception without judgment is spineless; judgment with no perception is blind. Introversion lacking any extraversion is impractical; extraversion with no introversion is superficial."[16]

Because of our innate preferences, the complementary team of our dominant and auxiliary processes normally copes with most of life's situations. In fact, the teamwork of these two most preferred processes is so preeminent in our personalities and in our lives that the traditional profiles of personality types are primarily descriptions of this duo working together. In the eight-process model, we normally link these processes whenever we talk about a specific type. The ENFP type, for example, is referred to as "Extraverted Intuiting with Introverted Feeling."

CONSCIOUSNESS AND UNCONSCIOUSNESS

When we think of who we are, especially the part of us that we like, we think primarily of that part of us that is conscious. We are consciously aware, automatically, of our conscious self. Behavior and mental activity that come through conscious mental processes can be intentionally controlled and adjusted.

Unconscious thoughts, ideas, and acts are subject to no such restraints. They are, by definition, beyond our control. The unconscious is the repository of subliminal information that was never consciously noticed, of repressed memories that are painful to deal with, and of the inherited memory of our evolutionary history.

Unconscious processes try to do what they are suited for, just as conscious ones do. Without regard for our conscious desires or intentions, our unconscious processes do their best to balance the biases of the perceptions and decisions of our conscious processes. However, because they have no conscious channels for expression, they are usually heard only indirectly—most commonly through dreams, through artistic endeavors, or in uncontrolled outbursts in times of stress. Because they are undeveloped, they usually express themselves crudely. Like a primitive artist without sophisticated tools or training, they draw their cryptic messages in the sand. We usually lack confidence and clarity about these messages. Often our conscious processes overrule them or drown them out. Becoming self-aware is largely about learning to recognize and embrace these vague communiqués from our shadow self.

Denied and repressed, unconscious processes can be a source of negativity and destructiveness. Accepted and brought into our awareness, they can bring balance, creativity, and wholeness to the human condition.

THE SEQUENCE OF THE EIGHT PROCESS PREFERENCES

The dimension of consciousness/unconsciousness affects how the position that a process occupies in a person's sequence of eight influences the role that process is likely to play. The further down the sequence the process is located, the less conscious it is likely to be and therefore the more compulsive, primitive, and negative its manifestations. In addition, each process's position relative to the other processes sets up dynamics of opposition, balance, and energy that also influence the characteristics of that position.

In the course of normal type development, middle-aged adults will typically have brought their three most preferred processes to a fairly high level of conscious control.[17] Processes five through eight will be mostly undeveloped and unconscious. The fourth will straddle the two psychic realms, thus earning the description "gateway to the unconscious."[18]

John Beebe has associated archetypal descriptors with the eight positions in order to help us understand the roles that the processes in those positions tend to play. It is outside the scope of this book to go beyond simply mentioning these descriptions (see appendix B). It is worth noting, however, that the first four archetypes carry connotations primarily of the supportive and positive roles that conscious processes tend to play, while the other four processes are associated with more negative representations, illustrating typical affects of undeveloped and unconscious processes. Processes that are observed in positions of high preference will tend to be recognizable from the descriptions we have given in this book. We do not want to confuse readers' introduction to process watching with descriptions of the more oppositional roles that our processes can manifest from the shadow side of our personalities. Once you become adept at recognizing the processes in their preferred positions, however, you will probably begin to notice how their primitive sides can show up as well.

APPROPRIATENESS

We generally employ an adept, less appropriate process over an undeveloped but more appropriate one. In a task focusing on collecting concrete data, like taking an inventory, for example, a person using his dominant Extraverted Intuiting might very well feel comfortable and appear competent in the work. But it is quite possible that his data is not actually as reliable as he believes it is. At the very least, the task will be quite draining. It will be very difficult for him to maintain a focus on the items being counted while engaging an Intuiting process. The individual may quickly tire from the constant intake of new, redundant data, being drawn to focus instead on exploring the patterns and possibilities implied in the data—the passion of Extraverted Intuiting. The continuous flow of new data may mushroom into a constantly changing explosion of possibilities. His focus on recording external information may wane quickly, and some of what he records may actually come from the patterns he perceives to be emerging from the data.

If this person instead manages to engage his more appropriate but less developed process of Extraverted Sensing in the task, the results may well be even less accurate or even inept if he has not developed a certain level of comfort and competence in using that process. Extraverted Intuiting is the dominant process for two personality types: ENTP and ENFP. For both, Extraverted Sensing is their least preferred process. In many situations, our more developed processes serve us better than more appropriate but relatively undeveloped ones.

A person in such circumstances also may have developed his or her Extraverted Sensing to some degree of conscious competence, despite its innately unconscious position in the sequence of preferences. Becoming comfortable and adept in using more and more of our processes is a lifelong task, called "individuation" or "type development," and "while the goal is wholeness and a healthy working relationship with the self, the true value of individuation lies in what happens along the way."[19]

Though type development can come about involuntarily through the circumstances of our lives, this can be traumatic and counterproductive. It is usually more beneficial to intentionally explore and practice the use of our undeveloped processes in a safe environment. It would probably be more desirable, for example, to develop Extraverted Thinking by presenting logical arguments in a classroom or at the dinner table than to avoid using the process altogether until we have to convince our company's board of directors to adopt a new marketing plan.

ENERGY FLOW

In a sense, the type model is all about energy. When you are process watching, look for the flow of energy. Is the person excited and drawing others into her enthusiasm? Is she low-key—perhaps even struggling and hesitant—and getting more and more drained as she goes along?

The energy-flow aspect of type is about the energy required for operating from a particular mental process. It is not, as some believe, simply about whether or not one is engaging in one's preferred energy-orientation attitude of Extraverting or Introverting. When we are operating in our favorite processes, we become more and more energized. We lose track of time and feel like we could keep going forever. On the other hand, using any process other than our dominant one creates internal tension and requires extra energy. Extra effort is needed to elevate the less comfortable process to the forefront and to keep the more familiar processes in the background. Even the auxiliary takes some energy to sustain at center stage. The lower a process resides in our preference sequence, the greater the effort that is required to employ it; even if it is reasonably well developed.[20]

Energy issues come into play in many ways. They can, for example, have an insidious effect on a relationship, even if an individual routinely makes an effort to use a nonpreferred process to meet another person in that person's preference. In this situation, though the two people may be using a common process, the person who is expending a lot of energy to do so may show his energy deficit by being slow or awkward. Even though he is actually making an admirable effort to communicate and relate, the other person, for whom the process is natural and easy to use, may become annoyed and alienated. She may make erroneous assumptions about why he is making the situation so difficult. This is the reason that in a conflict-resolution situation, it is more important that the participants meet on a level playing field, in terms of mental process preferences, than it is that any of them work from a process that is completely comfortable for them.

SUMMARY OF THE FACETS AND FACTORS

The following six points are the most important factors and dimensions of eight-process type. They are the keys to what you will observe and to what is going on beneath the surface:

* The nature of the eight processes themselves defines the limits of how they can operate and be manifested.
* The need for balance determines which processes can be drawn upon to effectively support and compensate for another process.
* Our psychic development, through individuation, brings our unconscious processes increasingly into useful, conscious control. The typical correlation of development with age helps explain the familiar stages of life that we all experience and observe.
* The innate sequence of process preference impacts the roles taken on by the processes and has broad influences upon the way in which our personal drama is played out.
* Energy flow impacts our ability to operate from our developed processes. It explains a great deal about why some activities "charge our batteries" while others drain them quickly.
* Appropriateness of the process to the situation sometimes influences which processes are used. It almost always influences how successfully they are used.

Complex and intimidating as this all may appear, the eight-process model actually allows us to savor the complex fruit of type at any pace that feels comfortable. It can be approached gradually by taking in just a little more with each bite—at first concentrating on the invigorating and accessible outer layer, process watching, then moving just beyond to experience the sweet richness that is its essence. Experienced type practitioners have expressed amazement at the depth of understanding that even new learners have quickly reached through this approach.

CHAPTER 14

BEYOND THE BASICS

In this chapter, we describe several kinds of situations in which type differences are known to play prominent roles. We focus on areas where knowledge of type can be particularly helpful. These are the areas where, in the near future, you may very well find yourself saying, "How did I ever do this before I understood type?"

Consciousness is the human being's individuation. Consciousness is the human being's flower.
Carl Jung

CONFLICT MANAGEMENT

Anne Singer Harris points out that "Jung believed that aggression on the collective level results from a failure to take responsibility for it at the personal level. He related this aggression to a refusal to recognize our own shadow [unconscious] aspect . . . . When we project . . . our deepest shadow . . . onto another person or nation, we see that person or nation as the cause of all our ills and disappointments. If the other does the same, soon we may be attacking each other in the name of making the world better. On the other hand, if each person learned to recognize and take responsibility for his or her own aggressive urges . . . the outside world would get less of the blame."[21]

The natural tension between the processes within each of us provides a needed push forward in our type development. But that healthy internal tension can quickly develop into external conflict when we encounter our own undeveloped unconscious processes in others. When we see people acting out the same tendencies that our conscious processes oppose within ourselves, the stage is set for friction, dysfunctional relationships, intolerance, and even war. For each of us, there are six types with which we are naturally most likely to clash, and these clashes will have different characteristics depending upon the particular conflict of mental processes that lies beneath the visible conflict.

It is necessary to look at people's entire sequence of eight processes in order to understand where the differences really lie. People whose four-letter type formulas look similar are not necessarily naturally compatible. Having the same dominant function in the different attitudes of Extraverting and Introverting, for example, is a common source of problems (e.g., ESTJ, dominant Extraverted Thinking, and ISTP, dominant Introverted Thinking). Perhaps this is because both types seem to be talking the same "language," yet their Introverting or Extraverting inexorably takes them in very different directions, with no obvious communication gap to help explain the split.

Many are surprised to learn that our psychological opposite is not a person with the type formula with the opposite letters (e.g., INTJ and ESFP); it is the one with the same attitudes and opposite functions (e.g., INTJ and ISFJ). Let's compare the process sequences of the INTJ, ESFP, and ISFJ types.

SEQUENCE OF PREFERENCES

E S F P   vs   I N T J

#	ESFP	INTJ	
1	Extraverted Sensing (Se)	Introverted Intuiting (Ni)	Conscious
2	Introverted Feeling (Fi)	Extraverted Thinking (Te)	
3	Extraverted Thinking (Te)	Introverted Feeling (Fi)	
4	Introverted Intuiting (Ni)	Extraverted Sensing (Se)	
5	Introverted Sensing (Si)	Extraverted Intuiting (Ne)	
6	Extraverted Feeling (Fe)	Introverted Thinking (Ti)	Unconscious
7	Introverted Thinking (Ti)	Extraverted Feeling (Fe)	
8	Extraverted Intuiting (Ne)	Introverted Sensing (Si)	

The pair of types that many have believed to be opposite, ESFP and INTJ, while they certainly have potential points of friction, also have a good chance of finding common ground. They can probably both consciously engage some mental processes where they can "meet" on a fairly equal footing in terms of the energy required, comfort level, maturity, and level of conscious control. If both of these people are at least middle-aged and have experienced normal type development, there is a good chance that they can come to communicate and work together reasonably well. They will probably have developed their four preferred processes to some level of conscious awareness, acceptance, and control. These types share the same four preferred processes in the conscious arena, though in reverse order of preference (see the diagram above). The most likely opportunity to find a level playing field for these two types lies in the languages and perspectives of Extraverted Thinking (Te) and Introverted Feeling (Fi).

SEQUENCE OF PREFERENCES

I N T J   **I S F J**

	INTJ	ISFJ	
1	Introverted Intuiting (Ni)	Introverted Sensing (Si)	
2	Extraverted Thinking (Te)	Extraverted Feeling (Fe)	*Conscious*
3	Introverted Feeling (Fi)	Introverted Thinking (Ti)	
4	Extraverted Sensing (Se)	Extraverted Intuiting (Ne)	
5	Extraverted Intuiting (Ne)	Extraverted Sensing (Se)	
6	Introverted Thinking (Ti)	Introverted Feeling (Fi)	*Unconscious*
7	Extraverted Feeling (Fe)	Extraverted Thinking (Te)	
8	Introverted Sensing (Si)	Introverted Intuiting (Ni)	

Now note the positions of the processes for INTJ compared to the positions for ISFJ. The processes are opposite images of each other. The archetypal roles of the different positions set up a myriad of likely points of friction (see appendix B). When someone with a preference for either of these types operates through his or her most preferred processes, he or she is acting in ways that the other type probably dislikes most and understands, respects, and trusts least. It is unlikely that either can consciously meet the other through shared concepts or language because the conscious processes of one are probably unconscious for the other. Between opposite types such as these, every process is a potential source of conflict. Appendix E, a circular type chart, shows the psychological opposite types on opposite sides of the circle.

In a sequence-to-sequence comparison matrix like the diagrams above, the closer the lines connecting the same processes are to being horizontal, the easier it will probably be for the types to understand each other's perspective and the better the chances are that the individuals will be able to communicate—if those processes are conscious. In the examples, we kept the diagram simple by drawing only the lines connecting each type's dominant and auxiliary processes to the same processes' positions in the other type. One could draw similar lines connecting all the like-processes. In the ESFP/INTJ comparison, we find a relatively level playing field between processes that are likely to be in the individuals' conscious control. But in the INTJ/ISFJ comparison, the only level field is between processes in the fourth and fifth positions—processes that neither individual is likely to have developed to a level of conscious usefulness.

It is important to note that an additional complication occurs whenever any of the introverted processes are involved because introverted processes are, by definition, subjective, personal, and unique. If the common ground between individuals is an introverted process, there is still a danger of a disconnect. Two people using Introverted Sensing, for example, could well have a totally different recall of an experience. Two people using Introverted Intuiting would likely associate very different visions and meanings with any given topic. Two people using Introverted Thinking probably have almost completely different internal frameworks and come at an issue in very different ways. Two people using Introverted Feeling may clash if they have different, conflicting internal values.

Another important potential source of conflict lies within normal, healthy type development itself. As a person develops a less preferred process into consciousness, he will initially engage the process very clumsily. Even after extensive practice, he will never be as sharp and skilled in using that process as someone who naturally prefers it and developed it early in life. The first illustration above diagrams the potential areas of friction when INTJ starts to tread on the psychological territory of ESFP. As the INTJ develops her third and fourth processes, Introverted Feeling and Extraverted Sensing, tension is created for the ESFP. Extraverted Sensing and Introverted Feeling are dominant and auxiliary for the ESFP. They are the processes that he knows best and trusts most. When the INTJ attempts to use these processes, they will not be as trusted or as skillfully employed as they are for ESFP. The relationship between the two people may have previously carried an unspoken understanding that INTJ is the vision expert and ESFP is the concrete details expert. Suddenly, the INTJ is noticing more about what is around her and may challenge the ESFP about a concrete detail. The ESFP may react with "Who does she think she is telling me about how the world looks? These are the things I have been trying to get her to notice since I've known her." Also, since the INTJ's venture into this new territory will be tentative and awkward, the ESFP may interpret it as being false and insincere. The same kind of conflicts could, of course, happen when the ESFP attempts to use his third and fourth functions of Extraverted Thinking and Introverted Intuiting. The balance, acceptance, and trust that had been established by these two when their type development was fairly stable may become unstable and tense when one invades the psychological territory of the other.

It is also worth noting the elevated role that Perception processes often play in creating and resolving conflict. Most of the long-term conflict in the world is tied to the differences in our approaches to Perceiving. Perhaps this is because when we try to understand and resolve these disagreements, we normally are focusing on decision making. We usually assume that everyone is starting with the same information, so the attention is on the conflicting choices being made, and we make assumptions about why others are making those choices. But, as we have seen, our information can in fact be very different, depending upon which Perceiving filters we use. One party may start from the history of the conflict: who did what to whom. Another may see the news of the day as the only relevant facts.

131

For a third participant, the specific possible courses of action, given the current situation, may be all he sees. Yet another party may come from the reality of a far-off vision of the future.

In such a situation, the root cause of the differences may not lie in the decision making at all. Before we can focus on making decisions, we first need to be aware of how the differences in Perceiving can give each of the participants a very different sense of the basic facts of the situation.

Managing conflict using the eight-process model starts with increasing the awareness among the players about the type dynamics that are at work. Ideally, everyone's preferred perception and decision-making processes should be shared by literally laying them on the table in an eight-process matrix for discussion, as in our two illustrations. The participants would start by sharing their preferred method of Perceiving, as described below:

- Extraverted Sensing: Talking about the concrete facts and what is going on at the present time with the conflict situation. "What do we know, as opposed to what we believe?" "What facts can all parties agree upon?"

- Introverted Sensing: Sharing relevant history and factual background information concerning the conflict. Providing a comprehensive, step-by-step, "First this happened, then he did that, then she did this . . . " accounting of the facts.

- Extraverted Intuiting: Exploring future possibilities. "What are other ways of managing the conflict?" "What different directions or endings can we imagine?"

- Introverted Intuiting: Looking at the "meaning" of the issue and at the distant effects. "When they do that, it means this." "This could come back to haunt us in ten years."

Once the parties come to an understanding about their perceptions, the next step would be to explore the decision-making process of each, as described below:

- Extraverted Thinking: Using quantitative tools such as decision trees, causal analysis, and matrices to logically sort and evaluate the known options for managing the conflict. "What facts, procedures, and goals can we agree upon?"

- Introverted Thinking: Weighing pros and cons and designing a decision-making process that would be most effective for managing the conflict. "What process would get us where we need to go?"

- Extraverted Feeling: Building harmonious relationships. "How is the conflict situation going to impact the people involved?" "What would be the human side of the various options?"
- Introverted Feeling: Seeing the values that drive the actions. "Are there violations of core values or beliefs behind the conflict?" "Do options for managing the conflict honor the core values of all the participants?"

In conflict resolution and conflict management, it is extremely helpful if all parties understand how the others are using their Perception and Judgment. Indeed, this is often the single most critical factor influencing success or failure. Without such an understanding, reconciliation attempts are uphill battles at best and hopeless exercises at worst.

Although the phrase "conflict management" may conjure up images of the epic conflicts of history and literature, understanding type holds the same kinds of benefits, and not understanding type holds the same hazards, for any relationship. The closer the relationship, the greater the potential impact of these dynamics. All positive, healthy relationships are built upon respect and appreciation. Whether the relationship is with a coworker, acquaintance, or life partner, learning about how each party perceives the world and makes choices is a direct route to that respect and appreciation and, in turn, to shared discovery and growth.

DECISION MAKING

Decision making is certainly not a discrete event or issue. It is an aspect of virtually everything we do. But many businesses have identified problem-solving or decision-making skills as a prime leverage point for improving organizational performance levels.

"The more one understands how each function works, the greater that individual's ability will be to make effective decisions."[22] In addition, the more mental processes that are involved in reaching a decision, the more balanced and sound that decision is likely to be. It is important to get information from all four Perceiving processes and input from all four Judging processes. When more than one person is involved, getting everyone's contributions will not only make it easier to reach that balance of processes, but it will also give everyone a vested interest in the decision.

In the following template for decision making, we have expanded upon four steps that were originally laid out by Isabel Myers[23] and which have become familiar to most type professionals as the "zigzag" analysis.[24] Most individuals or groups will find it difficult to effectively engage all eight processes as suggested below. However, by conscientiously following the eight steps, they can improve their ability to make better, more balanced decisions. The more we use each of the eight processes, the more familiar and comfortable it becomes. Remember, though, that no individual actually has conscious access to all eight processes. Even though they are all within us, affecting our behavior and our personality, some of our lower mental processes will forever remain unconscious. With good type development, though, we can recognize and value the processes that others use, even if we cannot consciously access some of those processes ourselves.

Using the eight-process model of type when you are making decisions can be extremely helpful both as a guide and as a teaching tool. We have included a brief, checklist version of the steps in appendix H as a "cheat sheet" to remind you to include all of the mental processes when making important decisions. We recommend that you follow it step by step, checking off each perspective that you consider before moving on to the next, until going through the entire sequence becomes a habit. Make an effort to give each step equal emphasis. If possible, get help with the steps with which you are impatient or uncomfortable from someone you trust in this area. Imitate the way people who seem energized by these steps approach them.

To demonstrate how the template could be applied, we include an example from the Community Garden Committee in the mythical city of Jungstown. The city makes plots of land available for gardeners who do not have their own gardening space. The committee has responsibility for overseeing the gardens in the Myersville neighborhood. At their annual fall meeting, they are assessing needs and making plans for next year, using the eight-process model to guide their decision making.

Step 1:
Gather concrete, current information.
(Extraverted Sensing)

A group is assigned to visit the city clerk's office and the garden site to document all the relevant information. The following is part of the list they produce:

- There are 294 households in Myersville.
- The available land is a rectangular area measuring 300 feet by 200 feet. It is divided into 100 plots, each measuring 30 feet by 20 feet.
- Most plots have been well maintained. A few are overgrown with weeds.
- Soil acidity is high (average pH: 6.0). Key nutrient levels are acceptable, except nitrogen is low.

To gather additional information, they recommend that a community-wide survey be conducted.

 Step 2:

Gather concrete information from past experience. Make comparisons and note what has worked and what has not. (Introverted Sensing)

Several longtime community gardeners on the committe contribute information from past seasons and draw comparisons with the most recent one.

- Interest has increased over the years. Last year, twelve applicants were turned away because there were not enough plots. The year prior to that, seven applicants were turned away.
- Friction has been growing between conscientious gardeners and those who let weeds and pests multiply. A few of the more experienced gardeners quit the program last year in frustration.
- Residents who are confined to wheelchairs have been unable to participate.
- The aesthetic quality and productivity of the gardens has gone downhill over the years.

They recommend that the past two years' gardeners be surveyed, asking what worked and what did not work for them.

Step 3:

Explore possibilities and options. Make connections to understand the "big picture."
(Extraverted Intuiting)

Starting with the information gathered in steps 1 and 2, this group brainstorms different options for responding to the issues.

- For accessibility issues:
    - ⇒ Create raised beds and better paths for wheelchair accessibility.
    - ⇒ Make tools like kneeling aids available to help people meet special physical challenges.
- For availability issues:
    - ⇒ Make some plots smaller to create more plots.
    - ⇒ Get more land for the gardens.
    - ⇒ Choose gardeners by lottery.
- For soil quality and garden productivity issues:
    - ⇒ Add lime and compost and rototill all gardens.
    - ⇒ Approach weed and pest control issues at a gardenwide level.
    - ⇒ Require a fee from all gardeners to fund improvements.
    - ⇒ Solicit volunteers for improvement projects.
- For friction issues:
    - ⇒ Reward conscientious gardeners and penalize careless gardeners.
    - ⇒ Hold a best garden contest.
    - ⇒ Establish rules and standards.
    - ⇒ Fit plot size to an individual gardener's ability to maintain it.
    - ⇒ Separate conscientious gardeners' and careless gardeners' areas.
    - ⇒ Let gardeners do whatever they want to do.

 Step 4:

Search within and beyond the information and ideas for relevant meanings, insights, and abstract associations.
(Introverted Intuiting)

The committee members explore the meaning of the various options. They search for significance and interrelationships beyond what can be documented or proved. They add these observations to the list.

Enabling older gardeners to participate opens up teaching/ learning opportunities for younger ones.	• Create raised beds and better paths for wheelchair accessibility. • Make tools like kneeling aids available to help people meet special physical challenges.
Customizing plot size and accessibility may help improve quality by discouraging gardeners from taking on more than they can handle.	• Make some plots smaller to create more plots. • Get more land for gardens.
A lottery would mean we would not truly be a community garden.	• Choose gardeners by lottery.
Unless we accept volunteer help as payment in kind for fees, we may not get enough help and we may exclude low-income people who need the gardens most.	• Add lime and compost and rototill all gardens. • Approach weed and pest issues at a gardenwide level. • Require a fee from all gardeners to fund improvements. • Solicit volunteers for improvement projects.
Some issues will never be resolved if approached on a piecemeal basis.	• Reward conscientious gardeners and penalize careless gardeners. • Hold a best garden contest. • Establish rules and standards.
The choice of whether on not to establish and enforce overall policies and standards represents a choice between restrictions and freedom and between higher standards and anarchy.	• Fit plot size to an individual gardener's ability to maintain it. • Separate conscientious gardeners' and careless gardeners' areas. • Let gardeners do whatever they want to do.

✓ Step 5:

Look at the interim steps and consequences of the possible alternatives. Choose one or more courses of action that appear workable and effective.
(Extraverted Thinking)

With all the information, options, and insights on flip charts, the committee discusses the logistics, practical steps, and consequences of various courses of action. Here is an abbreviated version of the result:

- Initiative A:
    ⇒ Approach some issues, such as pests, weeds, aesthetics, fertility, and accessibility, at the whole-garden level.
    ⇒ Establish minimum standards for responsible gardening.
    ⇒ Establish a team to inspect gardens and enforce standards.
    ⇒ Develop rewards and penalties.
- Initiative B:
    ⇒ Develop short-range and long-range improvement plans.
    ⇒ Solicit volunteer help for tilling and other tasks.
    ⇒ Apply for grants for tools, a shed, and more land.
    ⇒ Custom fit plot sizes to individuals.
    ⇒ Establish a supervisory team.
- Initiative C:
    ⇒ Ignore the issues.
    ⇒ Do not create an oversight committee.
    ⇒ Do not impose standards.
- Initiative D:
    ⇒ Create a separate new gardening area.
    ⇒ Separate conscientious gardeners' plots from careless gardeners' plots.
    ⇒ Lobby for support from the city government.

Using a matrix, the committee members analyze the proposed initiatives for their ability to address the key issues:

Initiative	A	B	C	D
Does it fit in our budget?	Yes	Yes	Yes	Yes
Do we have the manpower to do it?	Yes	Yes	Yes	Yes
Does it address accessibility issues?	No	Yes	No	Yes
Does it address availability issues?	No	Yes	No	Yes
Does it address soil quality and garden productivity issues?	Yes	Yes	No	Yes
Does it address friction issues?	Yes	Yes	No	Yes

 Step 6:

Determine a problem-solving approach.
(Introverted Thinking)

Detailed process maps are developed. For example:

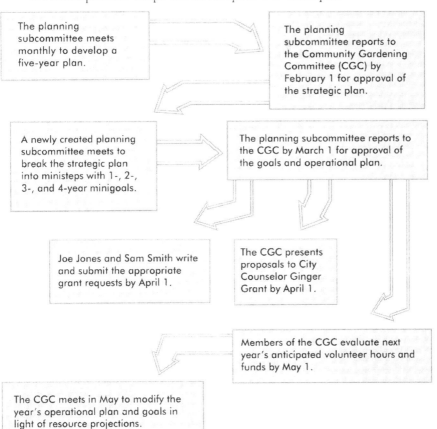

The planning subcommittee meets monthly to develop a five-year plan.

The planning subcommittee reports to the Community Gardening Committee (CGC) by February 1 for approval of the strategic plan.

A newly created planning subcommittee meets to break the strategic plan into ministeps with 1-, 2-, 3-, and 4-year minigoals.

The planning subcommittee reports to the CGC by March 1 for approval of the goals and operational plan.

Joe Jones and Sam Smith write and submit the appropriate grant requests by April 1.

The CGC presents proposals to City Counselor Ginger Grant by April 1.

Members of the CGC evaluate next year's anticipated volunteer hours and funds by May 1.

The CGC meets in May to modify the year's operational plan and goals in light of resource projections.

Step 7:

Check that the decisions and plans take care of the people who are involved as well as maintain good relationships within the community.
(Extraverted Feeling)

The Community Gardening Committee reviews and, if necessary, modifies the plans to ensure that they take care of the needs of the gardeners and the community and enhance the overall gardening experience. The following notes and modifications are added to the plans:

> Although establishing standards is in the best interest of all of the gardeners and will enhance the harmony of the experience, the CGC must make every effort to help the gardeners who fall below the standards. Rewards are to be emphasized over punitive measures. Education should be emphasized. For example, new gardeners may not understand how weeds spread. The committee should also determine whether gardeners need help due to illness, vacations, and such. Drastic measures should be used only when absolutely necessary for the greater good. A mentor network should be set up to help with education and to assist temporarily in cases of illness. Getting enabling tools and a shed should be a priority.

 Step 8:

Check that the proposed plans honor everyone's nonnegotiable personal values.
(Introverted Feeling)

With a complete, integrated plan provided ahead of time, the Community Gardening Committee asks its members to reflect on the decisions. They are asked to consider: "Does this feel right to me?" "Am I comfortable with this plan?" "Does it respect the needs and values of all the participants?" "Will any gardener feel excluded, ignored, offended, or hurt if we take these actions?" The members are then asked to bring any negative responses to the questions to the attention of the entire committee. The plan will then be modified or clarified, if necessary, to respect and incorporate these ideas.

Today's world values quick, decisive action. In business particularly, the individual who can deal with a constant barrage of emergency situations, taking them in stride and making decisions that solve the immediate problem, is viewed as a leader. We rarely take time to step back and evaluate the results of those decisions. If we did, we would see that most of the "brush-fires" that necessitate those snap decisions could have been avoided if earlier decisions had been more thoroughly thought through.

Although the eight-process approach illustrated above may seem cumbersome and lengthy, the more we can engage all the perspectives and tools that it provides, the less likely our decisions will be to produce unanticipated consequences. Obviously we cannot go through a laborious and difficult procedure for each of the hundreds of choices we make each day. But it is certainly worthwhile making the effort to begin to use this approach in making major decisions. The long-term efficiency will become clear to the careful observer as fewer and fewer unexpected consequences appear suddenly to require emergency meetings and "band-aid" decisions and detract from the effective and methodical work that moves us toward our goals. In addition, the more we become habituated to the eight-process approach, the more automatically we will come to use it in making all of our decisions.

COMMUNICATION

Improved communication follows improved understanding of type almost automatically. As our recognition of the mental processes sharpens, so too does our appreciation of the different perspectives offered and of the unique challenges faced in getting various insights across to others.

However, we do not need to limit ourselves to casual insights. We can apply ourselves quite effectively to improving our communication skills using the eight-process model of type. This has always been one of the principal benefits of familiarity with personality type, and probably no area that we could study is more important to our daily lives.

The context for communication is relationships. It takes at least two to communicate: someone to initiate the message and someone to receive it. Although passing information is certainly an important function of this interaction, much more is going on than a mere exchange of data. Verbally, we send messages in our tone, our rhythm, our choice of words, and many other intentional and unintentional ways. We send even more cues nonverbally through body language, facial expressions, focus of attention, energy level, and so on. Others pick up the bits and pieces of these messages that make it through the filters of their own perception and then they interpret them through their decision-making process bias. By the time something you are trying to say completes its journey to another person's awareness, it is as if it has been bounced between several funhouse mirrors. The message received may bear little resemblance to the one you thought you sent.

Think of the children's game called "telephone." Everyone sits in a circle and someone starts the game by whispering a specific sentence into the ear of the child next to him or her. Each child tries to pass the message to the next. By the time it has traveled around the whole circle, however, the message is always very different from the original one.

As an unknown author put it, "I know you believe you understand what you think I said, but I am not sure you realize that what you heard is not what I meant."

Messy and inexact as it is, communication is constantly and vitally important to us. Besides passing information, it is a big part of how we let others know who we are, and it is an essential part of building and maintaining our relationships. As we pointed out in our preface at the beginning of this book, relationships, flow of information, and self-definition are the key factors influencing the success or failure of all human systems—from life partnerships to corporations to nations. What, then, could be more important than improving our ability to communicate?

Like process watching in general, closely observing people's communication styles can teach us a lot about our differences and how to bridge the gaps. Below are some specific tips and insights regarding the eight distinct dialects of the mental processes. First, though, some general suggestions.

Keep in mind that communication is as much about receiving as it is about sending. In every communication, half of the Perceiving filters and half of the interpretive emphasis of Judging belong to the receiver. To improve our ability to communicate, we must focus as much on becoming aware of how our processes affect incoming messages as we focus on how they affect the outgoing ones. Below we emphasize our communication output for the sake of simplicity. But each point applies to our input as well. If our dominant process is Extraverted Sensing, we may tend to speak mostly in concrete, current facts. When we listen, we will also tend to focus on the parts of the information that relate to our sensory environment. People with an Introverted Intuiting preference, on the other hand, will tend to both speak and hear the meanings and abstract truths implied by the concrete facts but will probably pay little attention to the facts themselves. Unless people who prefer these two processes can learn to get a more complete and balanced message out and to let a more complete and balanced message in, most of the communication between them will be lost in translation.

Communication is at least as much about nonverbal messages as it is about the verbal ones. Research has repeatedly shown that in face-to-face dialogue, most of the information that comes across is nonverbal, and of the verbal message, most is not transmitted in the words. This is why for important, difficult interactions, face-to-face interaction is usually much more effective than a conference call, and e-mail is notoriously problematic. Effective communication involves a heightened awareness of demeanor, movement, timing, tone of voice, and energy level, just as much as the choice of words.

We send and receive messages all the time of which we are not aware. We can work to increase our awareness of the messages but will never achieve perfect communication awareness. It is important to always be mindful of what an inexact business communication really is. Watch for evidence of a disconnect. Are people still following what you are saying? Does someone seem suddenly put off? Ask questions for clarification. Get confirmation that you have been understood. Rephrase when you suspect that you have lost someone. Ask for others to rephrase back to you what they heard you say. Most of us tend to take communication for granted, but good communication is very hard work and well worth the effort.

It may be helpful to think of processes with which you are not familiar as speaking a different language from yours, or at least a strange dialect in which most of the words do not make sense to you. This is probably less of an exaggeration than our normal assumption that words have the same meaning to everyone and messages arrive intact from sender to receiver. The foreign language comparison helps remind us of the challenges we face. When people are not working through common, developed mental processes, serious translation obstacles need to be overcome before effective communication can happen.

Most teams gravitate quickly and tacitly to a certain mode of communicating. Leaders may set the example or the language may reflect the type bias of the group as a whole. If some members of a group are not fluent in the language being spoken, their options are limited. They can continue speaking in their own dialect, regardless of whether or not they are understood by others. They can try to use the language of an undeveloped process, making them uncomfortable and unlikely to succeed in getting their message across. More commonly, they simply will not participate, withholding their potential contributions and not buying in to the conversation or its results. None of these choices will accomplish effective communication unless the other participants help out. Imagine how different it would be if all of the members of the group learned to appreciate the value of the varied contributions and were willing to work to accommodate and understand the different languages that came with them.

Note that in the descriptions below, we are portraying how each process usually sounds when it is in the dominant position. Describing processes in the dominant position allows us to draw clearer and more recognizable distinctions between them. When a specific process is engaged but comes from lower in the preference sequence, even just one step down in the auxiliary position, the descriptions become more difficult to recognize. For example, when Extraverted Intuiting is the dominant mental process (ENFP and ENTP), it will sound similar to the description below. On the other hand, when Extraverted Intuiting is the auxiliary process (INFP and INTP), it may sound very different and be much harder to identify. Even though someone may be communicating through the auxiliary preference of Extraverted Intuiting, what is being communicated is usually coming mostly from her dominant process. You are probably hearing something that originates from her Introverted Feeling (INFP) or Introverted Thinking (INTP), reshaped as she extraverts through her Intuiting process. As you apply the descriptions of the pure processes below, try to keep in mind the different nuances created by the different ways these processes team up with others in the sixteen types.

EXTRAVERTED SENSING

The language of Extraverted Sensing tends to favor the present tense. Usually, a lot of physical activity accompanies the words—often constant movement of the eyes, hands, or feet, perhaps touching of objects in the environment. You will hear words that are very concrete and related to the five senses. There is quickness in the language. Those who prefer this process engage people with their friendliness and liveliness. Often it is hard for others to get a word into the conversation. The person's voice usually has an upbeat tone.

Those who prefer Extraverted Sensing love to tell stories. If you were to follow them around a party, you might hear the same story told five times to five different audiences, with new adaptations each time. They tell stories to make a connection to the present and to engage the people around them. They do not usually use metaphors or analogies. They like to interact with their audience and will quickly pick up and reflect the intonations and mannerisms of the people they are with. They often have a great sense of humor and like to be the center of the activity. The language is very literal.

You will notice that the communication style of people whose Extraverted Sensing is in the dominant position (ESTP, ESFP) has an engaging quality that connects with everyone. Of course, the tone of the communication is influenced by the auxiliary process of either Introverted Thinking or Introverted Feeling. Extraverted Sensing with Introverted Thinking (ESTP) will sound more objective and analytical, while Extraverted Sensing with Introverted Feeling (ESFP) will sound more soft and caring.

With people whose Extraverted Sensing is in the auxiliary position (ISTP, ISFP), you will hear their wit and notice that they pay close attention to those around them, but they have no need to be the center of the activity. When listening to people whose preference is for Introverted Thinking with Extraverted Sensing (ISTP), you may notice thoughtful pauses while they search for the precision and logic to support their interaction with the present environment. People who prefer Introverted Feeling with Extraverted Sensing (ISFP) will have thoughtful pauses too while they gauge the sincerity and authenticity of the people around them. The energy of the people around them can propel ISTP or ISFP types to become the life of the party, but usually for only a limited time.

INTROVERTED SENSING

The language of Introverted Sensing is concrete but also comparative. You will often hear phrases such as "looks like," "tastes like," "is similar to," and "remember when." You may notice a quiet time before people who prefer this process speak, as they remember and compare. They have a need to go inside themselves and check for a recollection that has some similarity to the subject at hand. Often the language is very sequential, and you can usually follow their complete thought process if you listen carefully. The language is concrete and provides examples and detailed descriptions to help others see what they are experiencing in their mind. Others may even notice changes in their facial expressions, tone, or body language as they re-experience the past.

If they tell a story five times, the story will remain factual and the same. They tell stories to let people know what has happened, not to get attention or to explain the significance of what happened. They are often not even aware of whether or not they are engaging the audience. The purpose of the story is simply to provide information about what was and to share an experience that relates to the current one. Beyond that, the point of the tale may be to note what worked or did not work in the past situation.

They may remain a mystery to others to some extent because their communications are often cut short. Other people often have difficulty listening to all the detailed comparative information. If the person who prefers Introverted Sensing anticipates being cut off or not listened to, he or she may not even attempt to join the conversation at all.

The stories and recollections of Introverted Sensing with Extraverted Thinking (ISTJ) will tend to have a logical connection to the subject that triggered the story and will be presented in an organized style.

Introverted Sensing with Extraverted Feeling (ISFJ) stories tend to have a connection or theme that reflects a focus on people. The story is likely to be recounted in the exact chronological order that it happened.

With Introverted Sensing as the auxiliary process (ESTJ, ESFJ), there is a tendency for people to start talking and find a connection with a past experience while talking. People who prefer Extraverted Thinking with Introverted Sensing (ESTJ) often present the logic first and then talk through the information as they think out loud. Those whose preference is for Extraverted Feeling with Introverted Sensing (ESFJ) often tell stories with direct connections or relevance to their audience.

EXTRAVERTED INTUITING

The language of Extraverted Intuiting has a characteristic quickness that is similar to that of Extraverted Sensing. It conveys a sense of movement and excitement. The subject matter that visibly energizes those who prefer this process usually involves possibilities or alternatives. Often they will not elaborate on the possibilities, just throw them out for others to grab and explore, attempting to engage others through discovering new and different ways to experience the environment. Though they usually start from something in the current world, they may jump past the connections or from one idea to another in a way that is both exciting and energizing but sometimes also confusing to others. They feel no need to fully discuss each possibility. Discussion of details is not interesting to them, and they would prefer to let others explore the facts and details. People who prefer Extraverted Intuiting see connections and patterns so easily that, to others, it will seem as if they make huge leaps as they move from information to options and from one option to the next. Often they assume that just one or two words are enough to convey each idea. Other people may become frustrated because often Extraverted Intuiting has difficulty stopping the generation of options to focus on facts and details. To help people with this preference in their communication, it may be helpful to make a clear distinction between when a meeting or discussion is in a data-gathering mode and when it is in a decision-making or problem-solving mode.

People with a preference for Extraverted Intuiting with Introverted Thinking (ENTP) tend to express possibilities in uncommonly precise language. They may even sound arrogant, as they seem to reword what others have said in order to make it more precise. When generating options, those who prefer Extraverted Intuiting with Introverted Feeling (ENFP) may sound more humane and caring, tending to emphasize how the possibilities would support people.

With Extraverted Intuiting as an auxiliary (INTP, INFP) one notices a quietness and a lower energy level in talking about possibilities. People who prefer Introverted Thinking with Extraverted Intuiting (INTP) usually need a quiet period of thought before they present a possibility or option aloud. They have a tendency to be very precise in their style of expression. They have thought a long time about exactly what to say and how to say it. With those whose preference is for Introverted Feeling with Extraverted Intuiting (INFP), you usually see a tone of easygoing gentleness with occasional bursts of energized passion, depending on whether or not the conversation relates to their core values. If those values are violated, however, either you will hear sarcasm and shortness or they may just withdraw from the conversation.

INTROVERTED INTUITING

The language of Introverted Intuiting is often very generalized and abstract and may seem totally disconnected from the external world. People who prefer this process tend to make statements that carry such a tone of conviction that the statements sound like decisions. However, they are really just pointing out information that others may not be aware of or see as connected to the topic being discussed. They often talk in metaphors about meaning or a vision of the future world. They may be hesitant to speak because their thoughts are very difficult to express in words that will be understood by others. If what they are talking about is important to them, you hear passion in their voice. The harder they try to explain, however, the more convoluted, abstract, and confusing their message will sound. They may even sound unintelligent in their struggle to communicate. Often they put forth an idea that is either not understood or not accepted at the time. Later, someone else may come up with the same idea but say it in more concrete terms and with more tangible evidence or examples, and it will be accepted. Introverted Intuiting often jumps too far ahead of the current environment for most people to relate to its insights or visions.

People who prefer Introverted Intuiting with Extraverted Thinking (INTJ) may sound abrupt, as if they give no consideration to the opinions and thoughts of others. They are actually attempting to talk out a decision with information that is still tentative and abstract. Those who prefer Introverted Intuiting with Extraverted Feeling (INFJ) also sound abstract but they tend to be more focused on what others are experiencing. As with INTJ, they are attempting to talk out a decision with information that they may not yet fully understand.

When the Introverted Intuiting is in the auxiliary position (ENTJ, ENFJ), there is more of a tendency to talk first and sort through the meaning or vision during the conversation. People whose preference is for Extraverted Thinking with Introverted Intuiting (ENTJ) use language that often sounds even more abrupt than that of the INTJ. They need to hear themselves in order to sort out what the images coming to them through their Introverted Intuiting mean. Their voice tends to have a very logical tone and it will often seem that they do not even care if others are listening. Those who prefer Extraverted Feeling with Introverted Intuiting (ENFJ) tend to talk about people and how the vision or meaning affects them.

EXTRAVERTED THINKING

The language of Extraverted Thinking serves a need to talk out one's thoughts. People who prefer this process need to talk in order to think. When listening to them, others may feel accosted by a barrage of thoughts. They are not really making judgments as they talk, but it often sounds that way. Though it sounds as if they are stating nonnegotiable conclusions, they are actually just throwing out ideas by extraverting their thought process in order to come to a conclusion. They often need others' responses in order to stimulate their own thoughts. But even if they get no responses, just having a forum in which to think out loud helps them to refine their analysis. You may even hear people with a preference for this process talking to themselves. They also enjoy debating, though others may see it as arguing. People with dominant Extraverted Thinking (ESTJ, ENTJ) should let others know that this is how they communicate. Otherwise, they run the risk of discouraging the give-and-take conversations that they are trying to stimulate. Others, especially subordinates, may run off to carry out what they assume to be decisions but are actually just ideas being worked out.

People who prefer Extraverted Thinking with Introverted Sensing (ESTJ) usually sound factual, analytical, and firmly grounded in the reality of a situation. Their Introverted Sensing process provides an abundance of facts and details for analysis and comparison. They seem to leave no room for considering other options or ideas, as if the decision has already been made. When they move from one topic to another it is usually through a shared logical connection.

Those whose preference is for Extraverted Thinking with Introverted Intuiting (ENTJ) usually sound quite abstract, and others may not understand exactly what they are trying to get across. Their need to think out loud, coupled with a content of those thoughts that others find difficult to relate to, can frustrate the people around them. The ENTJ tends to go in many directions at once. The movement from one subject to another is so swift that the thoughts may seem unconnected. Often it is hard for people with this preference to verbalize what the end result or goal will look like.

People who prefer Extraverted Thinking as the auxiliary process to dominant Introverted Sensing (ISTJ) have a tendency to search for relevant internal data first and then talk out the decision. The decisions do not sound as nonnegotiable as when Extraverted Thinking is in the dominant position. The communication of people whose Extraverted Thinking is the auxiliary process to dominant Introverted Intuiting (INTJ) can suffer from a scarcity of concrete information and examples. Although presented in a logical manner, INTJ's explanations tend to take enormous intuitive leaps, leaving gaps where others need specifics in order to understand and believe. The INTJ may lose credibility as they skip over details that they just know intuitively but cannot prove or explain.

INTROVERTED THINKING

The communication that others hear from people with a preference for Introverted Thinking is a summary of a logical analysis that has already been completed internally. You will not hear a half-baked thought. People with this preference need to think in order to talk. The length of the thought process depends on how well the topic fits into the personal logical framework that already exists in their mind. Their language is very precise, and sometimes they pause as they search for the exact word or phrase they need. Others may notice visible signals when this is happening. They often look as if they are actually doing a calculation in their head, and their eyes seem to focus on the internal task. They look distant, and often they are oblivious to the external world. Others do not see the detailed thinking that is going on internally as the person who prefers Introverted Thinking takes a journey in which precision is the goal. Often, their explanations sound more and more convoluted the harder they try to explain something. They may go off on what others see as tangents since their internal thought process is so personal and unique.

There is a tremendous difference between Introverted Thinking when it is supported by Extraverted Sensing versus by Extraverted Intuiting. People who prefer Introverted Thinking with Extraverted Sensing (ISTP) often come across as strongly opinionated: "This is my thought process, the facts are correct, the logic is precise, and so I am right. End of conversation." They also tend to come to closure quickly because they see what is there and are certain that that is all there is to consider.

Those who prefer Introverted Thinking with Extraverted Intuiting (INTP) tend to take longer to come to closure because they want to continue exploring possibilities and options. INTP often comes across as tentative. Others may even think that they have not been honest since it may seem as if they are constantly waffling or changing their mind. In fact, they are just explaining their thoughts. But as they do so, they continue to discover more possibilities or options.

For people whose Introverted Thinking is their auxiliary process (ESTP and ENTP), the communication styles resemble those of ISTP and INTP, but the influence of Introverted Thinking is far less visible. Most of what is noticeable will come from the dominant Extraverted Sensing or Intuiting. You can still hear the internal precision and logic, but the influence is very subtle.

EXTRAVERTED FEELING

The language of those who prefer Extraverted Feeling is full of "we" and "us." Even when they say "I," others often get the sense that they are reflecting a consensus, that they are speaking on behalf of everyone. They often start speaking abruptly, particularly when they are engaged in their favorite activity of promoting a cause or taking care of the underdog. Their language, like their activities, often gives the impression of a crusader charging off to do battle. At the same time, they usually exercise extreme care and skill in their choice of words and when to say them. Their priority of maintaining harmony between people can be a subtle business, and they tend to be good at being politically correct and not offending anyone. Their skill at conversation and managing situations is developed in order to fulfill the need to maintain harmony while constantly communicating and enforcing the rules of acceptable social behavior. Although others may not even notice, "shoulds" and "should nots" are either spoken or implied throughout their conversations. People who favor Extraverted Feeling tend to take care of the group, making sure that everyone has been introduced to everyone else, that everyone is heard, and that everyone is comfortable. They tend to have good radar for the emotional state of a group, and you may hear them reacting to that emotional component rather than to what has been said or done. They tend to move group processes quickly toward closure, sometimes too quickly for others. Since they tend to assume that they know what is best for the group, discussion is just a formality.

People who prefer Extraverted Feeling with Introverted Sensing (ESFJ) speak and act based upon past experience with what has and has not worked to create and maintain harmony around them. Their communication often focuses on others' physical health and on taking care of them. Actions will often accompany their words. At a party, you may see them offering people something to eat or drink at the same time they are attempting to solve the people-related problems of the world.

Those who prefer Extraverted Feeling with Introverted Intuiting (ENFJ) are more concerned about nurturing others' personal growth. They may recommend books or classes to help you in your personal development. They frequently become involved in organizations that promote these endeavors.

People whose Extraverted Feeling is the auxiliary process to dominant Introverted Sensing (ISFJ) immediately recall your last interaction, and they move quickly to fix any problem that happened or came to light during that previous experience. Those with Extraverted Feeling as the auxiliary process to dominant Introverted Intuiting (INFJ) have a tendency to focus on what may happen in a future interaction, rather than on what happened in the past. They will listen intently to you, but they may be listening for meaning behind your words rather than focusing on what you are saying.

INTROVERTED FEELING

The language of Introverted Feeling is the hardest to identify of all the processes, except on those occasions when a strong belief or value is being presented. Listening for the communication style of people who prefer the Introverted Feeling process is usually more about noticing what is not there than what is there. You will generally not hear an agenda, passion, well-reasoned or firmly defended positions, or "shoulds" and "should nots." They are often so agreeable, open, and willing to go with the flow that others may incorrectly see them as wishy-washy or without values. They never impose their values on others. If you pay close attention to them, though, you may notice that they exude a serene certainty that comes from knowing what is important to them.

When they do speak or act with an unusually high level of energy and passion, others' first reaction may be surprise at this seemingly uncharacteristic behavior. However, it is not really inconsistent or out of character. Only when their core values are threatened or otherwise engaged do the associated passion and conviction rise to the surface for others to see.

Sometimes their passionate defense of their values cannot be directly observed, as they may simply shut down and say nothing. Even in this situation, though, subtle hints can be heard in their words, and their body language is particularly expressive. They may sit a little straighter or even rigidly. More often than not, though, they will simply walk quietly and abruptly away from the person, job, or other situation that is in conflict with their values, with no explanation. This may seem like a total lack of communication. But the sudden exit and the refusal to discuss the matter further or to associate with the offending party clearly communicate a great deal, if you know what to look for.

Beyond the open, serene, easygoing nature that usually influences their tone, it is normally very hard to hear the voice of the Introverted Feeling process in these people. Often, most of what you hear is coming from their Extraverted auxiliary process.

People who prefer Introverted Feeling with Extraverted Sensing (ISFP) usually have an air of gentleness. They are at peace with themselves and they know who they are. They are not out to impress or influence others, so they tend to talk about what is actually happening right now. They speak in the present tense, and what you see is what you get.

Those who prefer Introverted Feeling with Extraverted Intuiting (INFP) show a peaceful face to the world. Only when they feel completely safe to express themselves will you hear the passion in their voice that reveals the true importance of certain things and people in their lives. They are not out to impress or convince others, and they focus on possibilities and options that support their value system.

People whose Introverted Feeling process is the auxiliary to dominant Extraverted Sensing (ESFP) possess a liveliness that may hide their deeply held values. They are usually fully engaged in their current environment, going easily with the flow except on those rare occasions when their core values are threatened. The passion of Introverted Feeling almost never is drawn to the surface where it can be seen or heard by others.

Those with Introverted Feeling as the auxiliary process to dominant Extraverted Intuiting (ENFP) also have a noticeable liveliness that usually hides their deeply held values. For ENFP, the outgoing, active focus is on generating and exploring possibilities that support people.

We cannot leave our discussion of communication without briefly mentioning another, closely related hot-button issue for organizations: teamwork. Everything that we have mentioned about communication can be directly applied to team building and team improvement. Addressing communication issues through the eight-process model of type will lead to changes at a far more fundamental level than by simply teaching some communication-improvement technique. Although improved listening and speaking techniques come with the package, the most important changes are the ones from which these visible improvements must spring—in areas such as trust, respect, and appreciation. Good communication is not the only ingredient essential to good teamwork, but addressing communication at this level addresses the other factors as well.

Through authentic, effective communication, individuals and teams can develop into powerful forces. Whether in a business partnership, a work team, or an intimate personal relationship, ineffective communication presents the most common and stubborn barrier to success and happiness for all relationships. With the depth of understanding and appreciation of each other's gifts that can be attained through communication improvements that are guided by an understanding of type, the team itself can become a more complete entity, drawing adeptly on its collective array of developed mental processes. Together the individuals can reach a level of completeness beyond anything that we are likely to reach individually. They become a substantial force in all their mutual endeavors, while together they move closer to the sense of wholeness that we all seek.

It is certainly possible to have an effective team without a conscious awareness of type. But by approaching team building through teaching about type, we are promoting a natural process of personal development in all the participants. Not only can the team itself become significantly more effective, but the team members can become more balanced, effective, and fulfilled in virtually everything they do. The time and effort spent laying the groundwork by familiarizing the group with the basics of type usually produces a return on the investment very quickly and with results that can be dramatic. Most leaders who have witnessed what this knowledge can accomplish would not even consider working without it ever again.

MANAGING CHANGE AND TRANSITION

Change management has become a hot issue in the past decade because technological advances have created a global economy in which businesses have discovered that agile adaptability is vital to success.

- Businesses increasingly outsource work that had previously been done in-house, creating an epidemic of transition shock.

- Customer expectations may shift suddenly and you have to re-engineer your product or service overnight.
- Your information system is upgraded and everyone has to suddenly change how they work without missing a beat.
- A merger throws completely different corporate cultures together, creating chaos, while stockholders expect that the new organization will immediately be stronger than the sum of its parts.

But handling transition is actually something that we humans do rather well. Without this ability to adapt, our species would not have survived to evolve into the highly complex organisms that we have become. The complexity and diversity of our social structures bear witness to our ability to innovate in our relationships as well. We have evolved in a world where change is constant, not an occasional and temporary condition that happens between stable situations. As individuals, we all have effective ways of adapting—whether to dramatic changes, like our first day of school or the loss of a loved one, or to normal daily upheavals at work, like shifting priorities and daily "brushfires."

In *a simpler way*, Margaret Wheatley and Myron Kellner-Rogers point out that "The resistance we experience from others is not to change itself. It is to the particular process of change that believes in imposition rather than creation." Organizations can most effectively manage change and transition by taking advantage of their employees' individual adaptability, allowing and enabling them to cocreate the necessary new reality. Unsuccessful transitions are always the result of overmanaging or undersupporting this natural process. Rather than trying to control transition, leaders can best contribute by first defining boundaries and then attending to whatever the individuals and teams need in order to do their jobs. This is where an understanding of type can be a tremendous boon.

People with different process preferences have different needs and will use different approaches in dealing with change. Below is a quick look at how these needs and approaches work.

PERCEIVING

People with different Perceiving preferences need to know different kinds of information to make a decision:

- Extraverted Sensing:
    - ⇒ How is this change affecting me now?
    - ⇒ How is this change affecting the organization now?
- Introverted Sensing:
    - ⇒ How does this change compare with changes I have experienced in the past?
    - ⇒ How does this change compare with previous changes in the organization?
- Extraverted Intuiting:
    - ⇒ What are the possibilities for me?
    - ⇒ What are the possibilities for the organization?
- Introverted Intuiting:
    - ⇒ What does this change mean for me?
    - ⇒ What does this change mean for the organization?

JUDGING

People with different Judging preferences use different ways of making the decisions required for adapting.

- Extraverted Thinking:
    - ⇒ Is there a logical order and rules or standard procedures to guide the change effort?
    - ⇒ Does this external logic mesh with mine? Can I see the logic?
- Introverted Thinking:
    - ⇒ What will be the process of the change?
    - ⇒ Is the process fair and well conceived and does it fit my subjective logical framework?
- Extraverted Feeling:
    - ⇒ How are the people in the organization going to be impacted by the change?
    - ⇒ How is my family going to be impacted by the change?
- Introverted Feeling:
    - ⇒ Does this change create a conflict with my value system?
    - ⇒ Will this change support my value system?

157

Take, for example, a look at the story of Moses through the lens of type.

Moses had a vision. He knew what needed to happen and he could see the result in his mind's eye. His challenge was to communicate that vision to his people in a way that would inspire them to abandon their familiar lives as slaves in Egypt and embark on a long and dangerous journey. Moses, in this version of the story, preferred Introverted Intuiting. This abstract, visionary mental process enabled him to know with certainty that freedom awaited the Israelites in a place he thought of as the Promised Land. But when Moses talked about the Promised Land and tried to persuade the people to follow him, no one got excited. No one wanted to follow him. He went alone to the desert and spent considerable time contemplating why this was so. Like many otherwise great leaders in today's corporate world, Moses had a vision but his abstract way of communicating presented a serious problem.

The key to Moses's success was his type development. It enabled him to realize that he was simply not communicating in a way that everyone could understand. He needed to change his language to help his people visualize the Promised Land too. By simply changing the phrase "Promised Land" to "The Land of Milk and Honey," he was immediately able to rally all the Israelites behind the vision. Through this simple change of translating his abstract vision into concrete, tangible terms, Moses provided useful information for each of the data-gathering and decision-making processes.

The people with a preference for Extraverted Sensing needed information about how the change would affect their current lives and environment in tangible ways. They would follow Moses because it would impact them immediately. When they cleaned the plates of the Egyptians, they tasted the food that had been left on the plates. They vividly understood the difference between what they were given to eat and what the Egyptians were having. They were the first to say, "We will follow you so that we can eat good food."

The people with a preference for Introverted Sensing needed information that they could relate to through past experiences about tangible things that they could compare to the present. Though they may never have had milk and honey to drink and eat, their grandparents had described these delicacies in vivid stories about the good old days. They remembered the elders talking about how, long ago, they were never thirsty and they always had enough to eat. This reminded them that, in the stories, their grandparents and great-grandparents had also spoken fondly of freedom. Freedom and plentiful good food and drink were obviously superior to gruel, water, and slavery, and they wanted to experience this better life. So they too were ready to follow Moses to the Land of Milk and Honey.

Those whose preference was for Extraverted Intuiting needed information that held a promise of new, exciting options for the future. They talked about this Land of Milk and Honey and about everything they could do with milk and honey. They could make cakes, pies, and many other delicious foods. They followed Moses because they could do a lot more than just drink milk and eat honey. A whole new world of possibilities and options would be open to them.

The people with a preference for Introverted Intuiting needed information that would evoke abstract visions of what the future could be like. They bought in to the idea of the journey because for them the concept and imagery of a Land of Milk and Honey carried associations of what freedom really meant. For some, it meant security and it conjured up images of a safe place for their children to grow and live in freedom. For others, it meant an end to degradation and fear, as they would never have to wait on someone else or worry about being hungry.

Note that each of the Perception processes has a very different time focus. In order to appeal to everyone, Moses needed to use imagery that people could relate to through the past, present, and future. (See appendix I.)

Those people with a preference for Extraverted Thinking needed to see a concrete goal. "The Promised Land" had not been specific enough. When Moses provided an end result that was tangible, the Land of Milk and Honey, they were able to logically discuss the goal versus their current living conditions. They then made the decision to follow him and to work together to attain that goal.

The people with a preference for Introverted Thinking saw the logic in making a move from slavery to being free and well fed. Before they were ready to go, they each met with Moses and explained their thoughts on how they would go about leaving, as well as the entire process that would be necessary in order to make a successful journey.

Everyone with a preference for Extraverted Feeling could see that living in their own land of plenty would bring harmony to the tribe. Everyone else was going to follow Moses. The journey would be made with family and friends. They would be together in this new Land of Milk and Honey. Of course they wanted to be a part of this great social event.

Most of the people with a preference for Introverted Feeling held a core value that slavery was wrong. Others had experienced gut-level discomfort with some aspect of their lives in Egypt: humiliation, not having enough to feed their children, and so on. To be in a new land where all could be true to themselves would give them a sense of internal peace.

When Moses found language that could energize all personality types, through the ways they each preferred to take in information and make decisions, everyone jumped on board and they were off to the Land of Milk and Honey!

PARENTING AND EDUCATION

Understanding type is an incredibly powerful aid for parenting. Type-knowledgeable parents of young children are constantly telling us that they cannot imagine raising their children without this understanding. Those who learned about type later in life are always saying, usually with a big sigh, how much they wish they had known then what they know now.

In *Gifts Differing*, Isabel Myers passes along a true gem of insight about child development. She summarized this insight when she observed that "What children need is the conviction that satisfaction can and must be earned. Parents who value this conviction can give it to their children, but the parents must start early and remember both the 'can' and the 'must.'"[25] Her observations are particularly relevant in today's society, where, for many of us, giving our children almost anything they want is no longer thought of as spoiling them, where punishment is out of fashion and tough love is such a novel concept that it needs a label, while at the same time many other children suffer lives of neglect and are abandoned to the streets.

Myers points out that, starting at a very early age, type development takes place as we learn effective ways to take in information and to make choices that are based on that information. We need to have both successes and failures to encourage us to move toward the approaches to Perceiving and Judging that work for us and avoid those approaches that do not. Normally, we start life experimenting with a wide range of tactics, then focus and refine these approaches as we learn what produces more desirable results. If this feedback loop is broken, if a child does not experience both success and failure, that child lacks both the motivation and the information needed for healthy type development.

Myers said that a child who is rewarded no matter what she does never learns the critical lesson that "satisfaction . . . must be earned." On the other hand, a child that rarely experiences success from his choices may never learn that "satisfaction can . . . be earned." Though the circumstances of these two childhood scenarios are essentially opposite, the results can be surprisingly similar. Neither receives the mix of experiences that tells him or her, "That approach worked; try it again next time" and "That did not work; try a different approach next time." This is the typical feedback that would normally turn children's experiments with coping tactics into lessons for the development of their information-gathering and decision-making strengths. Instead, both learn that what happens in their lives is out of their control. It is someone else's fault.

Without the balance of responses to their choices that nurtures healthy type development, the likely long-term result is an unbalanced and unusually low level of type development. They will probably not possess the comfort and skills with a balanced toolkit of processes at the various stages of life that Grant leads us to expect (appendix C). As adults, they may cope with life well most of the time, but when a situation calls for anything beyond their limited personality toolkit, they will be unable to adapt. If the task changes from one that involves nails to one requiring screws and you notice that someone is still using a hammer, no matter how skillfully, then you may be witnessing severely limited type development in action.

Perhaps less dramatic, but very common, is parents' inability to recognize and value a child's innate process preferences. In a family where a preference for Extraverted Thinking prevails, for example, a child's natural Introverted Feeling process may be discounted. Throughout his formative years, such a child may be given the consistent message that his gut-level values are not important because they don't "make sense."

This situation will typically have one positive effect in that the child will attain some comfort with and conscious awareness of his third or fourth process well ahead of the normal developmental timetable. In the example of the innate preference for Introverted Feeling, the child may develop some skill and comfort in using Extraverted Thinking. If the pressure of this family bias is strong enough, however, the damage will far outweigh the benefits. In our example, neither the innately preferred Introverted Feeling nor any other Judging process is likely to ever be developed to the high level of competence that it could have attained through normal development. In addition, the stage is set for a battle between the natural, albeit repressed and less effective approach to decisions and the processes that the child has been taught should be used. The result may be a lifetime of identity confusion, inner conflict, and underachievement. This battle is also one of the common causes of inaccurate reporting through the Myers-Briggs Type Indicator® and similar personality type instruments.

"When each child is given the freedom to use the strengths of his or her psychological type without constraint, then development is steady, sound and secure. Parents and teachers are the people who have the greatest influence on children, and it is important that the differences in psychological type in children be recognized both at home and at school. Type differences appear to have a profound affect on early learning and indeed appear to have an impact on almost every area of life."[26]

The *MBTI® Manual* notes that "Professionals in this area [using type assessment with children] generally advise caution in specifying a type for young and preadolescent children, as there may be wide variation in the developmental process for individual children. Nevertheless, counselors and therapists who treat young children often find that the hypothesized type of a child may be related to the child's presenting problems."[27] In other words, information about type can be very useful for working with children, but only if one is very careful to take into account how unique this phase of normal personality development is, how misleading behavior at this age can be, and how difficult it is to draw reasonably reliable conclusions about children's innate process preferences.

From the perspective of the eight-process model, we would do well to take this same cautious approach when working with individuals of any age. It is true of adults, too, that understanding a process that is being used at any given moment may well be more fundamental to counseling than knowing whether or not it is innately preferred (i.e., reflective of their true type). Knowing an individual's true process preferences is an extremely valuable piece of the puzzle of personality, but in order to understand what is going on with that individual, it is often more crucial that we understand the process he or she is using in the moment.

Of course, this is especially applicable to youngsters who are at an age when they are actively experimenting with various approaches to Perceiving and Judging. In therapy and counseling for a child who is thoroughly engaged in exploring and developing a certain mental process, the best place to start is probably by understanding where that child is. Knowing whether she would prefer to be elsewhere (i.e., whether her innate preference will probably ultimately lead her to more thoroughly develop another process) may or may not also be helpful with the issue at hand. In dealing, for example, with a first grader's behavior problem of never sitting still and not paying attention in class, it would be extremely useful to understand if he is just going through a normal phase of exploring his Extraverted Sensing process, interested, at this time, only in exploring the world around him. It would probably be far less relevant to this situation to know that his natural preference is for some other process.

In the United States, our school system suffers from an institutionalized process bias. Preschool and kindergarten typically focus on external stimulation (Extraverted Sensing). Children are encouraged to explore colors and shapes through drawing. They build tangible objects like collages and mobiles. They physically interact with their environment through play. They sing songs, notice what lives in ponds, and find out what earthworms taste like.

Grades one through two encourage the socialization that appeals to Extraverted Feeling and Introverted Sensing. Encouraged activities and behavior include making friends and engaging in many different kinds of group activities. Children experiment with being mean to others. In all these relationships and interactions, they are exploring what works and what does not work for them with other people. The focus is on socialization.

Grades three through five emphasize the logical, predictable relationships between concrete things, using the kind of information that is naturally gathered through Introverted Sensing and working with that information using the analytical tools preferred by Extraverted Thinking. By categorizing their discoveries and learning to file away information for further reference, children can bring a whole new level of understanding to everything they experience. Previous experience and known information can thus be carried over to the new, dramatically increasing children's ability to expand upon new knowledge. Tadpoles are understood to be baby frogs. Trees, as a group, are understood to be different from flowers, and pines are different from maples. Even in their first encounter with an oak tree, these children can quickly understand a lot about it because they have learned that it is likely to be more like a maple than a daisy.

Grades six through ten push the Extraverted Intuiting process by emphasizing connections and different possibilities. Students are introduced to the ambiguity of interpreting poetry. They get to make choices between different options for elective studies that allow them flexibility in their learning.

In grades eleven and twelve, the Introverted Intuiting process starts to come into play with the emphasis on theory for college-bound students, adding a sense of meaning and purpose to what is experienced. Students learn to project and extrapolate from a known piece of information forward to imagine future possibilities and backward to hypothesize explanations of how things came to be as they are.

At the junior-high and high-school levels, Extraverted Sensing, the world of the tangible, is the focus for those on a vocational track. These students learn to observe and manipulate materials and tools to create furniture, houses, solar automobiles, airplanes, and soufflés. They learn to use data, software, and hardware to create computer games, databases, and movies.

College continues in the direction of the abstract and theoretical that favors Introverted Intuiting. At this level, students are being trained to see underlying patterns, connections, and meanings in order to fully appreciate the theories and constructs that form the foundation of their chosen fields. Even technical colleges and the more practical curricula require high levels of theoretical understanding. It is not enough for a civil engineer to know the mechanics of bridge design. She needs to understand the theories involved so she will be able to design a bridge that meets a novel technical challenge with a novel design and still know that it will not fall down. Likewise, to perform at the top level, musicians, visual artists, auto mechanics, computer programmers, and librarians all are trained in this way as a tool for fully bringing their talent and technical skills to fruition.

This preset, institutionalized progression of emphasis on exercising certain mental processes works reasonably well for most of us. But it is hardly ever a perfect fit for anyone throughout their entire time in the system. Most of us can remember a period or two when school itself just was not any fun. We often hear people make statements like "I really hated third grade." Our public education system, as it currently exists, was modeled after the factory. Its student-to-teacher ratios, approaches to grading and advancement, relatively inflexible curricula, and accompanying process bias, all serve to deliver a moderate level of education to a lot of people—to be efficient. Despite the heroic efforts of most educators, the structure of the system itself is virtually incapable of the flexibility that would be required to deliver a great education to anyone. At any point when children's innate preferences are at odds with the prevailing process bias of the school system, they will not be capable of taking in much of what is being taught in class. Nor will they be getting the valuing and validation of their preferred processes that is needed to encourage their personal development.

CAREER DEVELOPMENT

Why do so many of us work in jobs that do not fill many of our needs—jobs that drain our energy and leave us feeling frustrated and dissatisfied? Why do we spend most of our lives earning a living to support the very different lives that we may lead on weekends?

When we make career decisions, we often fail to understand the real nature of a job. If we decide that we want to be a firefighter, we may picture fighting fires and saving lives but may not think about the other 99 percent of our work life that we will spend at the firehouse. We may desire an executive's stature and income and the excitement of making important decisions, but what about feeling responsible for so many people? What about spending most of our life in meetings?

Finding out what a career path or specific position is really like and what psychic resources are required is crucial to our long-term professional success and happiness. But that is the relatively easy part. Any competent career counselor and scores of books can help you understand the true nature of the work. The bigger challenge is to discover your own true nature so that you can make a good match. For understanding your talents, how you prefer to operate, and what is really most important to you there is no better tool than the eight-process model of personality type. Many career counselors and several books approach career choice through type, although nothing is currently available on careers that incorporates the eight-process model. Career decisions made without understanding our process preferences are very likely to be poor ones. Type knowledge is virtually indispensable in this arena. "The use of the Myers-Briggs Type Indicator® personality inventory in career counseling to help people find meaningful and productive work was one of Isabel B. Myers' original motivations in the development of the instrument (Saunders, 1991). Career counseling applications were one of the first areas of applied research on type, and the field continues to generate a large number of research studies."[28]

We do not subscribe to the notion that people should seek positions and employers should hire based on the "ideal" type for the work. Not only would such a practice violate the ethical standards for the use of personality type instruments, but it really would not work well for the organization or its employees either. The result of such a practice could fail to challenge individuals to stretch to develop their less preferred processes. For the organization, the result would be workforce segments that lack the rich insight and agility that a mix of process perspectives can give, as well as teams that would probably have a very hard time dealing with other teams. Type can help your career choice, not by prescribing certain vocations for certain types, but by giving you insights into your needs and strengths. Understanding your preferred processes, particularly your dominant one, can best be used, not to find some theoretically perfect, tailor-made job, but rather to find a job that somehow supports your preferences. This is the kind of fit that produces much more satisfied and valuable employees. Approach career decisions with the insights of type, but do not feel constrained by those insights.

An accountant with preferences for Introverted Intuiting with Extraverted Feeling (INFJ), for example, would be unusual in her field. But her natural abilities to abstract and conceptualize and to relate to others' needs may make her a great teacher of accounting. On the other hand, she needs to be aware that the daily focus of her work—taking in concrete data and manipulating it according to specific rules—draws heavily upon less preferred processes. She needs to understand the energy drain that this causes and develop tactics to deal with it.

A human resources director with preferences for Extraverted Thinking with Introverted Intuiting (ENTJ) and a well-developed fourth process (Introverted Feeling) learns to leverage his ability to home in on individual employee's needs and values and to treat them as unique individuals by helping them take care of those needs and values. By supporting his employees in this way, he is able to free them from their focus on meeting their own needs and enable them to refocus their work on the needs of the organization. This is not the conventional approach, and it would probably not be the approach of a stereotypical HR manager, but it works very well indeed for this HR manager.

The career development checklist below is a thumbnail version of some key preference-related factors to take into account when choosing a career. Respecting the needs and focus of your dominant and auxiliary processes is crucial to finding satisfaction in your work life.

In the workplace, a person who prefers Extraverted Sensing tends to
❑ Excel in work that is realistic, tangible, and practical
❑ Enjoy contributing as a reliable source of accurate concrete information
❑ Need external stimulation from events, people, and objects in order to feel energized and effective

In the workplace, a person who prefers Introverted Sensing tends to
❑ Flourish in an environment that provides consistency and stability
❑ Lend stability to the organization and team by providing an historical

perspective on current events and an orderly, sequential approach to work processes
❏ Need to be involved in tasks, work processes, and situations that are familiar in order to feel comfortable and energized

In the workplace, a person who prefers Extraverted Intuiting tends to
❏ Be energized by generating new pragmatic options and possibilities
❏ Need personal autonomy and organizational flexibility that encourages trying new ideas
❏ Want to be surrounded by people who can become excited by new ideas and will work to bring them to fruition

In the workplace, a person who prefers Introverted Intuiting tends to
❏ Excel at providing long-range vision for effective strategic planning
❏ Enjoy work and contribute best when allowed to operate independently and given a great deal of creative license
❏ Need work that provides a sense of meaning and purpose

In the workplace, a person who prefers Extraverted Thinking tends to
❏ Thrive on work that involves using external objective criteria for logical analysis
❏ Need opportunities to "talk out" decisions with coworkers
❏ Be energized by creating order in work systems and procedures and in the physical environment of the workplace

In the workplace, a person who prefers Introverted Thinking tends to
❏ Need autonomy in decision making and have difficulty changing conclusions in the moment, through debate or discussion
❏ Contribute detailed approaches for addressing complex issues and projects
❏ Need private time in order to pursue inner understanding through extensive subjective analysis

In the workplace, a person who prefers Extraverted Feeling tends to
❏ Thrive in an environment that encourages supporting and interacting with people

❑ Want to contribute by promoting and defending the social values of the organization

❑ Need to work for an organization that supports employee growth, well-being, and success

In the workplace, a person who prefers Introverted Feeling tends to

❑ Be energized by work that aligns with his or her core values and supports an organizational mission that also aligns with those personal values

❑ Contribute by lending moral stability to the workplace and team

❑ Need a work environment that supports his or her inner harmony and values

Like the other life issues highlighted in this chapter, career development is an area where an understanding of personality type can be a particularly powerful tool. By taking into account our needs and finding ways to cultivate and use our gifts, we dramatically increase the likelihood that our life at work will be productive and fulfilling.

C. G. Jung subjected the human psyche to an empirical scientific scrutiny that was, perhaps, both more daring and more thorough than has been done by any other individual before or since. He followed the evidence wherever it led and, with appropriate humility, did his best to grasp and then explain a vitally important realm of the human condition that was not only virtually unknown but is in many ways unknowable.

Katharine Briggs and Isabel Briggs Myers took Jung's theoretical constructs and, in effect, democratized them. They created a practical tool for enhancing self-management and mutual understanding that can be used by virtually anyone in the world. They were so painstaking and thorough in their work that the richness of their insights and the applications of psychological type are still being rediscovered today.

Many hundreds of dedicated individuals have followed the lead of these pioneers by laboring to understand and expand upon the theory and its practical applications.

The authors see the model that we call "eight-process type" as another in a long tradition of efforts to facilitate human beings' ability to know themselves. We see this as a goal that becomes more and more urgent as humanity's capacity to destroy itself continues to leap ahead of its maturity. It is because we have seen the usefulness of this model in making type more readily available—at a greater depth of self-understanding—to more people that we seek to explain and promote its use.

If you too find it informative, useful, and exciting, we encourage you to continue your journey of discovery by exploring the information resources listed in the bibliography and recommended reading list.

We hope that your journeys will be fulfilling and that our paths will cross again.

JUNG'S MODEL OF THE PSYCHE

Throughout his adult life, C. G. Jung thought and wrote about the different aspects of human psychology that revealed themselves to him through his psychoanalytical practice. Assembled all together, these bits and pieces describe a comprehensive model of all the phenomena and activities of our mental life: our psychic energy system, personality, thoughts, and emotions as well as their visible products, our traits and behaviors. Collectively, these mental mechanisms and activities are called the psyche.

Below is a graphic representation of Jung's model of the psyche, showing very simplistically how the pieces fit together. Although we do not explain this overall psychic system or most of its individual parts in any detail in this work, you can get some hint of how it all meshes together by looking in the glossary at the definitions of the terms used in the illustration.

The mental processes of personality are shown in their positions of consciousness and unconsciousness as we would expect to find them in normally developed adults according to Beebe's theory. Note that the first four are located to varying degrees in the conscious, while the lower four are immersed entirely in

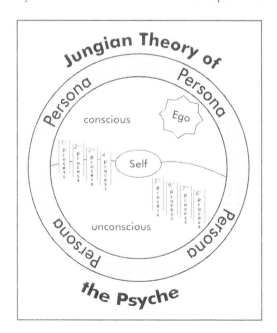

the unconscious. We have pointed out that the psyche is a system of energy and balance. As long as the processes remain in their natural positions, the personality is in balance. We rely, as naturally as breathing, on our most conscious processes—primarily our first and second. But as we engage processes from further and further down our preference sequence, more and more psychic tension is created and more and more energy is required.

Picture the psyche as a crystal sphere half filled with water. The water represents the unconscious and the air filling the upper half represents the conscious. Floating in the water at the different depths shown in the illustration are eight elongated ice cubes representing the eight processes. They are at rest, requiring no energy to stay where they are. However, raising them higher into consciousness or pushing them deeper into unconsciousness does require energy. The further we move them and the longer we hold them in an unnatural configuration, the more energy is needed.

If we continue holding our personality in such a state of tension and imbalance for prolonged periods, we become less able to cope with the mental and physical demands of our lives. Our mind/body has less energy available to properly continue with its normal activities and maintenance functions. We may become aware of this energy drain and call it "stress." If we come to understand its root cause—a personality system that is chronically out of balance—we will probably think of it in terms such as "trying to be someone other than who we really are." Eventually, our depleted energy system may even allow physical disease conditions to take hold. Maintaining the natural balance of our psychic energy system is crucial to our health. Allowing our processes to play roles in our lives that are appropriate to their innate positions is a big part of that psychic balance.

Continuing with our ice and water analogy, imagine moving the ice cubes gracefully out of their normal positions and then back. With good type development, we become increasingly able to make such smooth transitions when they are needed: suppressing our preferred processes and bringing others to the surface of our consciousness to help us deal with the circumstances of our daily lives while accepting messages from unconscious processes when they ask for our attention.

On the other hand, if we push processes up or down violently or desperately hold them down until they burst to the surface, we create waves and splashes. This turbulence affects our entire psyche.

Smooth, appropriate, temporary shifts from the preferred positions of the illustration are normal and healthy. The sudden, ill-timed, unintentional eruptions that can result from thrusting the processes into unnatural positions or expending excessive energy to hold them in place for extended periods are not only not healthy for us, they can become manifest in our lives in dysfunctional, embarrassing, and dangerous ways.

JOHN BEEBE'S ARCHETYPAL UNDERSTANDING OF PSYCHOLOGICAL TYPES

In John Beebe's model, the sequence of the eight mental processes is not so much a hierarchy of preferences as simply a key to understanding the character and purpose with which each individual process will operate within each of the sixteen personality types. Although each of us has a dominant function or process that is natural for us to "default" to, various factors lead us to use each of the other processes at different times. When we bring a process other than our naturally dominant one into consciousness in order to tap into its resources, we are essentially bringing it temporarily into the "dominant" position and suppressing all the others. Like holding basketballs underwater, a considerable amount of strain is involved in keeping them somewhere that is not their natural position in the equilibrium of the system. A significant amount of energy is required to bring a process into consciousness "over" the others and to maintain it there. Tension is created in the psychic system. This tension is both necessary for growth and a potential cause of internal and external conflict.

Beebe was one of the first to present a convincing argument that the environmental attitude of the third (and seventh) process is opposite from that of the second (and sixth).[29] In addition, he has made tremendous contributions to our understanding of how the position of a process in the sequence of eight affects the role it plays in personality. These roles appear to be ancient templates within our collective unconscious that have been ingrained through the course of our psychic evolution. They are, in other words, archetypes.

Dr. Beebe's eight archetypes are summarized together here for your convenience. In several places, where other Jungian analysts have written about the same archetypes, he uses Latin or mythological names for these classic, unchanging ways of being human, to emphasize their archaic character. More information about each archetype can be found in the glossary. Here they are listed in the order that corresponds to the sequence of process preferences. Beebe speaks of each archetype "carrying" the corresponding process. The Hero/Heroine carries the first process, the Father/Mother carries the second, and so on.

1. The Hero/Heroine (usually the same gender as the individual): The top authority. We place unqualified trust in the Hero/Heroine and depend upon it without reservation. We use the process that is carried by this archetype to take care of ourselves—particularly our ambitions and goals.
2. The Father/Mother (usually the same gender as the individual): Living up to the model of the idealized parent, it focuses on taking care of others. It is supportive and nurturing and also sets a standard of perfection. The process that is carried by this archetype acts as the right hand to the dominant process and is often seen as the older and more mature of the two.
3. Puer/Puella (usually the same gender as the individual, though often with androgynous characteristics): Like a child, this classic archetype of eternal youth often serves to moderate the purposefulness of the dominant/auxiliary team, enabling the person to "lighten up": to play, be silly, be creative, make mistakes, become charming and eager to please. *Puer* and *puella* are Latin words for "boy" and "girl." The process that is carried by this archetype is often seen as a less mature and more irresponsible side of the person.
4. Anima/Animus (usually the opposite gender from the individual): Appreciative of the characteristics of someone of the opposite gender to the point of idealization. These names for its two sides are Latin words for "soul" and "spirit." Since the process that is carried by this archetype is opposite in both function and attitude to the dominant, it complements the first process, acting as a "backseat driver" to remind the dominant of what it is not taking into account. Good development of the process that is carried by the Anima/Animus is extremely valuable in providing maturity, balance, passion, and perseverance.

5. The Opposing Personality (usually associated with a figure or state of mind of the opposite gender from the individual): This is the first of the four archetypes associated with process positions that remain mostly unconscious in normally developed adults; as Jungian analysts say, they remain "in shadow." The process that is carried by the Opposing Personality often serves as either a passive or aggressive adversary both to the Hero/Heroine and also to other people, sometimes defending us but often criticizing us internally and throwing us off balance.

6. The Senex/Witch (usually the same gender as the individual): As the second process acts to advise and nurture, the process carried by the sixth archetype seeks to discourage, cast doubt, and set limits, often in a somewhat authoritarian, stern, and arbitrary manner. *Senex* is Latin for "old man." Its wisdom is hard to understand and at worst it simply gives very bad advice.

7. The Trickster (usually the same gender as the individual): Can operate very much like a rebellious, mischievous child—tricking and confusing and deviously trying to get its own way. The process that is carried by this archetype can sometimes help us to overcome arbitrary or unreasonable obstacles. The Trickster compensates for the vulnerability of our Eternal Child, enabling us to better survive the cruelty of the world.

8. The Demon/Daimon (usually the same gender as the individual, but being deeply unconscious, it can be represented by either gender, by animals, and even by inanimate objects): This is frequently the most problematic of all the archetypes. The process that is carried by this archetype usually operates in a manner that is undermining to others and to oneself. It is capable of gross distortion, causing confusion and chaos, and disrupting trust.

ARCHETYPE	TYPE PROCESS	CONSCIOUS/ UNCONSCIOUS	GENDER (variable)	PURPOSE
Hero/Heroine	Dominant	Conscious	Same gender as individual	Organizes adaptation; initiates individuation
Mother/Father	Auxiliary	Conscious	Same gender	Nurtures and protects others; sets standard of care
Puer/Puella	Tertiary	Conscious	Same gender	The endearing, vulnerable child in us that copes by improvising
Anima/ Animus	Fourth	Conscious	Opposite gender	Gateway to the unconscious; source of ideals that are difficult to live up to
Opposing Personality	Fifth	Unconscious	Opposite gender	Defends by offending, seducing, or avoiding; provides self-critiquing
Senex/Witch	Sixth	Unconscious	Same gender	Defends by refusing, belittling, and inactivating; sets limits
Trickster	Seventh	Unconscious	Same gender	Mischievous; creates double binds; circumvents obstacles
Demon/ Daimon	Eighth	Unconscious	Same gender	Undermines self and others; creates opportunities to develop integrity

TWO IMPORTANT CONTRIBUTIONS FROM HAROLD GRANT

Those who work with type are aware that there is an ongoing debate over the attitude of the third function. Independently from but more or less simultaneously with John Beebe, Harold Grant began speaking of the issue in the early 1980s. They both had found that their observations pointed to the third function being in the opposite attitude from the second.[30] Furthermore, this conclusion seems consistent with one of the cornerstones of all of Jung's psychological constructs: just as water inherently seeks to be level, the various dimensions of the psyche always seek a state of balance. Our own experience and a growing body of evidence collected by other practitioners and researchers appear to support this conclusion. We have used this model throughout our work. For those who are skeptical, we urge you to test it as an hypothesis within the eight-process framework. We are convinced that your clients will have far more success in verifying their true type and developing their own psychic versatility with this model.

Grant also put forward a timetable for normal development of the four preferred processes of type based on his own empirical observations. This template is not by any means absolute. But we have found it to be a very useful rule of thumb for typical, normal development.

As we have noted in the section on parenting (chapter 14), many factors, some of them quite common, can influence type development. These environmental influences alter the normal pattern of development outlined in the table. In these cases, however, it is still very useful to be aware of the innately preferred sequence and timetable of process development.

It must also be noted that full individuation, bringing all eight processes completely into consciousness, is a theoretical ideal. It is what businesspeople might call the ultimate "stretch goal." Jung repeatedly pointed out that humankind simply has not evolved to be able to handle that level of consciousness. The processes in the fifth through eighth positions in our sequence of preferences are parts of ourselves that we may develop with some success in our later years, as noted on the chart. But the further down we go in our preference sequence, the more difficult and uncomfortable the individuation becomes, and the less likely it is that we will ever bring the process to any significant level of comfort and control.

Grant's timetable for bringing the innately unconscious processes into consciousness is illustrated below. We have expanded the table, based on Beebe's work, to include the four mental processes that are more difficult to bring into awareness.

TYPICAL AGES FOR DEVELOPMENT OF PROCESSES (APPROXIMATE)	GRANT'S DEVELOPMENTAL TIMETABLE				BEEBE'S ADDITIONS			
	6–12 YEARS	12–20 YEARS	20–35 YEARS	35–50 YEARS	OVER 50 YEARS	OVER 50 YEARS	OVER 50 YEARS	OVER 50 YEARS
ISTJ	Si	Te	Fi	Ne	Se	Ti	Fe	Ni
ISFJ	Si	Fe	Ti	Ne	Se	Fi	Te	Ni
INFJ	Ni	Fe	Ti	Se	Ne	Fi	Te	Si
INTJ	Ni	Te	Fi	Se	Ne	Ti	Fe	Si
ISTP	Ti	Se	Ni	Fe	Te	Si	Ne	Fi
ISFP	Fi	Se	Ni	Te	Fe	Si	Ne	Ti
INFP	Fi	Ne	Si	Te	Fe	Ni	Se	Ti
INTP	Ti	Ne	Si	Fe	Te	Ni	Se	Fi
ESTP	Se	Ti	Fe	Ni	Si	Te	Fi	Ne
ESFP	Se	Fi	Te	Ni	Si	Fe	Ti	Ne
ENFP	Ne	Fi	Te	Si	Ni	Fe	Ti	Se
ENTP	Ne	Ti	Fe	Si	Ni	Te	Fi	Se
ESTJ	Te	Si	Ne	Fi	Ti	Se	Ni	Fe
ESFJ	Fe	Si	Ne	Ti	Fi	Se	Ni	Te
ENFJ	Fe	Ni	Se	Ti	Fi	Ne	Si	Te
ENTJ	Te	Ni	Se	Fi	Ti	Ne	Si	Fe

BRIEF DESCRIPTIONS BASED ON THE TWO PREFERRED PROCESSES

The following thumbnail portraits of the sixteen types are created from descriptions of their dominant and auxiliary processes. These are certainly not intended as complete descriptions of the types, merely as a convenient quick reference tool. They should also encourage readers to begin to consider the ways that these processes work together to create the sixteen types.

ISTJ	ISFJ
Introverted Sensing	Introverted Sensing
• Past experience through the five senses	• Past experience through the five senses
• Subjective historical perspective and comparison to the present	• Subjective historical perspective and comparison to the present
• Re-experiencing impactful events, people, and objects	• Re-experiencing impactful events, people, and objects
with Extraverted Thinking	with Extraverted Feeling
• Objective use of criteria and analytical tools	• Objective, external, people-oriented values
• Organization of the external world for logical analysis	• Maintaining social and moral standards
• Clarity, order, and competence	• Harmony in the environment

ISTP	ISFP
Introverted Thinking	Introverted Feeling
• Subjective framework of principles and categories	• Subjective, nonnegotiable core values
• Cause-and-effect analysis	• A centered, nonjudgmental serenity
• Logical precision	• Inner harmony
with Extraverted Sensing	with Extraverted Sensing
• Present environment through the five senses	• Present environment through the five senses
• Broad, detailed, accurate, and objective observation	• Broad, detailed, accurate, and objective observation
• Fully present here and now	• Fully present here and now

ESTP	ESFP
Extraverted Sensing	Extraverted Sensing
• Present environment through the five senses	• Present environment through the five senses
• Broad, detailed, accurate, and objective observation	• Broad, detailed, accurate, and objective observation
• Fully present here and now	• Fully present here and now
with Introverted Thinking	with Introverted Feeling
• Subjective framework of principles and categories	• Subjective, nonnegotiable core values
• Cause-and-effect analysis	• A centered, nonjudgmental serenity
• Logical precision	• Inner harmony

ESTJ	ESFJ
Extraverted Thinking	Extraverted Feeling
• Objective use of criteria and analytical tools	• Objective, external, people-oriented values
• Organization of the external world for logical analysis	• Maintains social and moral standards
• Clarity, order, and competence	• Harmony in the environment
with Introverted Sensing	with Introverted Sensing
• Past experience through the five senses	• Past experience through the five senses
• Subjective historical perspective and comparison to the present	• Subjective historical perspective and comparison to the present
• Re-experiencing impactful events, people, and objects	• Re-experiencing impactful events, people, and objects

INFJ	INTJ
Introverted Intuiting	Introverted Intuiting
• Subjective use of the contents of the unconscious	• Subjective use of the contents of the unconscious
• "Sixth sense" awareness	• "Sixth sense" awareness
• Meaning and abstract interrelationships	• Meaning and abstract interrelationships
with Extraverted Feeling	with Extraverted Thinking
• Objective, external, people-oriented values	• Objective use of criteria and analytical tools
• Maintaining social and moral standards	• Organization of the external world for logical analysis
• Harmony in the environment	• Clarity, order, and competence

INFP	INTP
Introverted Feeling	Introverted Thinking
• Subjective, nonnegotiable core values	• Subjective framework of principles and categories
• A centered, nonjudgmental serenity	• Cause-and-effect analysis
• Inner harmony	• Logical precision
with Extraverted Intuiting	with Extraverted Intuiting
• Objective generation of options and possibilities	• Objective generation of options and possibilities
• Connecting data in the past, present, and future	• Connecting data in the past, present, and future
• Tangible connections and possibilities on a global scale	• Tangible connections and possibilities on a global scale

ENFP	ENTP
Extraverted Intuiting	Extraverted Intuiting
• Objective generation of options and possibilities	• Objective generation of options and possibilities
• Connecting data in the past, present, and future	• Connecting data in the past, present, and future
• Tangible connections and possibilities on a global scale	• Tangible connections and possibilities on a global scale
with Introverted Feeling	with Introverted Thinking
• Subjective, nonnegotiable core values	• Subjective framework of principles and categories
• A centered, nonjudgmental serenity	• Cause-and-effect analysis
• Inner harmony	• Logical precision

ENFJ	ENTJ
Extraverted Feeling	Extraverted Thinking
• Objective, external, people-oriented values	• Objective use of criteria and analytical tools
• Maintaining social and moral standards	• Organization of the external world for logical analysis
• Harmony in the environment	• Clarity, order, and competence
with Introverted Intuiting	with Introverted Intuiting
• Subjective use of the contents of the unconscious	• Subjective use of the contents of the unconscious
• "Sixth sense" awareness	• "Sixth sense" awareness
• Meaning and abstract interrelationships	• Meaning and abstract interrelationships

THE CIRCLE OF EIGHT-PROCESS TYPE

When the process preference sequences of all sixteen types are laid out in a circle, their relationships to one another can be easily observed. Notice that each type's opposite is directly across from it, on the opposite side of the circle.

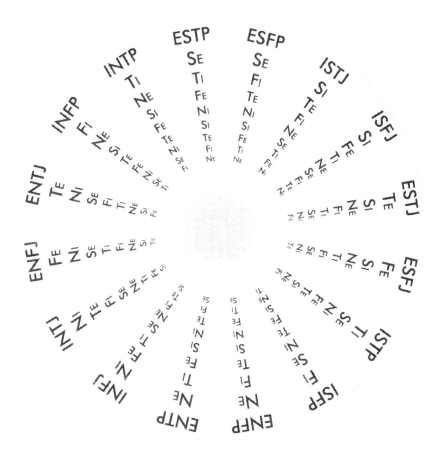

COMPARISON OF JUNGIAN MENTAL PROCESSES

Here is another quick reference tool for you. It contrasts features of each process with those of the process that has the same function in the opposite attitude.

EXTRAVERTED SENSING (Se)	INTROVERTED SENSING (Si)
• Is about objective perceptions	• Is about subjective perceptions
• Experiences the factual external data of the environment	• Experiences factual data in the form of detailed memories
• Experiences objective reality through the five senses	• Records objective reality gathered through the senses
• Reflects on the current physical world	• Reflects on internal impressions of the past
• Relates to the intensity of the physical world in real time	• Relates to the intensity of previous experiences
• Focuses on external objects	• Focuses on internal memories
• Experiences the world as an immediate sensation	• Experiences the world as a precise recollection

EXTRAVERTED INTUITING (Ne)	INTROVERTED INTUITING (Ni)
• Is about objective possibilities	• Is about subjective meanings
• Perceives aspects of physical reality	• Perceives aspects of psychic reality
• Uses the external environment of people and objects as triggers	• Uses the environment and unbidden contents of the unconscious as triggers
• Converts what is into what could be	• Converts what is into meaning and symbolism
• Generates endless new opportunities from the environment	• Generates new meanings through insights from the unconscious
• Changes existing objective situations into possibilities through concrete connections	• Changes existing or future situations through inner images
• Sees the potential of what is in the present	• Sees what is to come in the future with a sense of certainty

EXTRAVERTED THINKING (Te)	INTROVERTED THINKING (Ti)
• Is about objective analysis	• Is about subjective analysis
• Is motivated by outer reality to bring order to life	• Is motivated by inner ideas to bring precision to life
• Focuses on external facts and objects (extensity)	• Focuses on internal images and concepts (intensity)
• Establishes order in the environment	• Establishes clarity and precision in the mind
• Adopts criteria for decision making from logical constructs in the environment	• Adopts criteria for decision making from logical internal constructs
• Depends on external debate and analysis to reach conclusions	• Depends on internal analysis to reach conclusions

EXTRAVERTED FEELING (Fe)	INTROVERTED FEELING (Fi)
• Is about objective values	• Is about subjective values
• Follows generally accepted social values and norms	• Follows internal standards and ethics
• Is motivated by a sense of the worth of others	• Is motivated by private core values
• Creates harmonious conditions in the environment by attending to the emotions of others	• Creates harmonious conditions within by attending to one's own emotions
• May sacrifice one's own values in order to avoid offending others	• Will follow one's own value system regardless of the consequences
• Strives for rapport with others	• Strives for inner peace

PROCESS/ARCHETYPE CHART FOR THE SIXTEEN TYPES

This quick reference tool shows the sequence of process preferences for each of the sixteen types, along with the archetype that carries each process.

	ISTJ	ISFJ	INFJ	INTJ	ISTP	ISFP	INFP	INTP	Beebe's Archetypes
Dominant	Si	Si	Ni	Ni	Ti	Fi	Fi	Ti	Hero/Heroine
Auxiliary	Te	Fe	Fe	Te	Se	Se	Ne	Ne	Mother/Father
Tertiary	Fi	Ti	Ti	Fi	Ni	Ni	Si	Si	Puer/Puella
Fourth	Ne	Ne	Se	Se	Fe	Te	Te	Fe	Anima/Animus
Fifth	Se	Se	Ne	Ne	Te	Fe	Fe	Te	Opposing Personality
Sixth	Ti	Fi	Fi	Ti	Si	Si	Ni	Ni	Witch/Senex
Seventh	Fe	Te	Te	Fe	Ne	Ne	Se	Se	Trickster
Eighth	Ni	Ni	Si	Si	Fi	Ti	Ti	Fi	Demon/Daimon

	ESTJ	ESFJ	ENFJ	ENTJ	ESTP	ESFP	ENFP	ENTP	Beebe's Archetypes
Dominant	Te	Fe	Fe	Te	Se	Se	Ne	Ne	Hero/Heroine
Auxiliary	Si	Si	Ni	Ni	Ti	Fi	Fi	Ti	Mother/Father
Tertiary	Ne	Ne	Se	Se	Fe	Te	Te	Fe	Puer/Puella
Fourth	Fi	Ti	Ti	Fi	Ni	Ni	Si	Si	Anima/Animus
Fifth	Ti	Fi	Fi	Ti	Si	Si	Ni	Ni	Opposing Personality
Sixth	Se	Se	Ne	Ne	Te	Fe	Fe	Te	Witch/Senex
Seventh	Ni	Ni	Si	Si	Fi	Ti	Ti	Fi	Trickster
Eighth	Fe	Te	Te	Fe	Ne	Ne	Se	Se	Demon/Daimon

DECISION-MAKING CHECKLIST

You may want to use this summary as a reminder to use each process when making important decisions. Use it often enough, and it will become a very beneficial habit.

- Extraverted Sensing (Se)
  - ❏ Concrete data
  - ❏ Here and now
- Introverted Sensing (Si)
  - ❏ Subjective recall
  - ❏ Experience
- Extraverted Intuiting (Ne)
  - ❏ Connections
  - ❏ Seeing new possibilities and the big picture
- Introverted Intuiting (Ni)
  - ❏ Meanings and hunches
  - ❏ Insight
- Extraverted Thinking (Te)
  - ❏ Objective, logical criteria within a visible structure
  - ❏ Goal focus
- Introverted Thinking (Ti)
  - ❏ Principles and truth within a precise internal framework
  - ❏ Process focus
- Extraverted Feeling (Fe)
  - ❏ Social values and norms
  - ❏ Interpersonal relationships
- Introverted Feeling (Fi)
  - ❏ Personal values
  - ❏ Internal harmony

TIME FOCUS OF THE PERCEIVING PROCESSES

Jung says, "There are truths which belong to the future, truths which belong to the past, and truths which belong to no time."[31] The four Perceiving processes each pay attention to different parts of the time continuum.

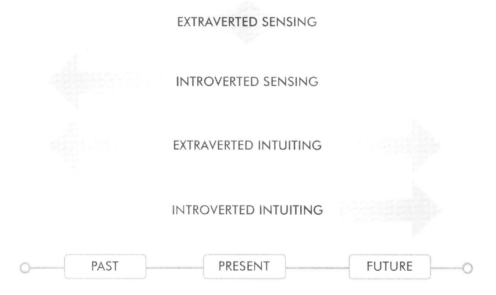

EXTRAVERTED SENSING

INTROVERTED SENSING

EXTRAVERTED INTUITING

INTROVERTED INTUITING

PAST — PRESENT — FUTURE

The time focus of Extraverted Sensing is on the present. Its awareness is of the current environment, noticing a broad range of concrete information in detail. It is the most reliable source of sensory facts about the environment.

The time focus of Introverted Sensing is on the past. It relates to the present and future through a subjective, comparative review of past experiences. It provides a historical perspective that can improve current and future endeavors based on its sequential recall of exactly how things have been done in the past and what worked and what did not.

The time focus of Extraverted Intuiting is broad, encompassing the past, present, and future. Although often starting from new information in the present, its search for what can be done with the new information quickly leads to tangible connections to both the past and future. It generates future possibilities with demonstrable connections to the past and present.

The time focus of Introverted Intuiting is on the distant future. Though usually lacking in detail, its vision encompasses an almost infinite scope of factors that are not limited by great separations in time and distance. By making abstract leaps from minimal concrete data, it can provide insight into the broad, long-term effects of current courses of action.

NOTES

1. Isabel Briggs Myers with Peter B. Myers, *Gifts Differing: Understanding Personality Type* (Palo Alto, CA: Davies-Black, 1995), 27.

2. Ibid., 77.

3. Leona Haas, Robert McAlpine, and Margaret Hartzler, *Journey of Understanding* (Palo Alto, CA: CPP, 2000).

4. Gary Hartzler and Margaret Hartzler, *Functions of Type: Activities to Develop the Eight Jungian Functions* (Huntington Beach, CA: Telos Publications, 2005).

5. Carl G. Jung and M.-L. von Franz, eds., *Man and His Symbols* (Garden City, NY: Doubleday and Co., 1964), 304.

6. Myers, *Gifts Differing*, 175.

7. John Beebe, *A New Model of Psychological Types*, audiotape no. 317 (Chicago: The C. G. Jung Institute of Chicago, 1988).

8. Carl G. Jung, *Psychological Types* (Princeton, NJ: Princeton University Press, 1976), 516.

9. Daryl Sharp, *Personality Types: Jung's Model of Typology* (Toronto: Inner City Books, 1987), 91.

10. The fourth aspect of what we now know as personality type was implied in Jung's work, but it was Katharine Briggs and Isabel Briggs Myers who developed the understanding of it as a dichotomy that provides the key to identifying our sequence of process preferences.

11. Carl G. Jung, *Psychological Types*, trans. H. G. Baynes, rev. R.F.C. Hull (Princeton, NJ: Princeton University Press, 1976), paragraph 913.

12. Sharp, *Personality Types*, 91.

13. Ibid., 65.

14. It should be noted that the environmental dichotomy simply provides a piece of key information needed to reveal an individual's process preferences. Like the other dichotomies, it provides very little useful information alone, standing separate from the rest of the system. For this reason, those who understand the eight-process view of type tend to avoid making generalized statements about Judging types or Perceiving types as groups. Eight type codes contain a J as the last letter and eight contain a P as the last letter. The Judging types are almost as different from each other as they are from the eight Perceiving types. Likewise, the Perceiving types are nearly as different from each other as they are from the eight Judging types.

15. Beebe, *A New Model of Psychological Types*.

16. Myers, *Gifts Differing*, 174.

17. W. Harold Grant, Magdala Thompson, and Thomas E. Clarke, *From Image to Likeness: A Jungian Path in the Gospel Journey* (Mahwah, NJ: Paulist Press, 1983).

18. John Beebe, *A New Model of Psychological Types*.

19. Daryl Sharp, *C. G. Jung Lexicon: A Primer of Terms and Concepts* (Toronto: Inner City Books, 1991), 69.

20. Whenever people try to understand any form of energy, in any context, they are confronted with apparent contradictions. The physicist, in explaining the nature of light, for example, must use two seemingly conflicting models, particle theory and wave theory, to explain all of light's properties. The paradox within the energy-flow aspect of type is that it seems to be about both *expending* and *taking in* energy. Although it is difficult to grasp how both can be going on at the same time, we can clearly observe that there is always an energy-flow factor. The lower a process is in our sequence of preferences and the longer we engage that process, the more extreme our net loss of physical, mental, and even spiritual energy becomes. Likewise, the higher the process we are using, the less draining the experience. In fact, engaging our dominant process usually has an energizing effect.

21. Anne Singer Harris, *Living With Paradox: An Introduction to Jungian Psychology* (Pacific Grove, CA: Brooks/Cole Publishing Co., 1996), 7.

22. Katharine Myers and Linda Kirby, *Introduction to Type Dynamics and Development: Exploring the Next Level of Type* (Palo Alto, CA: CPP, 1994), 32.

23. Myers, *Gifts Differing*, 197.

24. Term coined and popularized by Gordon D. Lawrence, people types & tiger stripes (Gainesville, FL: CAPT, 1979).

25. Myers, *Gifts Differing*, 197.

26. Charles Meisgeier and Elizabeth Murphy, *Murphy-Meisgeier Type Indicator for Children: Manual* (Palo Alto, CA: CPP, 1987), 1.

27. Isabel Briggs Myers, Mary H. McCaulley, Naomi L. Quenk, and Allen L. Hammer, eds., *MBTI® Manual: A Guide to the Development and Use of the Myers-Briggs Type Indicator®* (Palo Alto CA: CPP, 1998), 239.

28. Ibid., 285.

29. John Beebe, "Psychological Types in Transference, Countertransference, and the Therapeutic Interaction" (paper presented at the Chiron Conference, Ghost Ranch, NM, 1983).

30. Grant, Thompson, and Clarke, *From Image to Likeness*.

31. Carl G. Jung, *The Collected Works of C. G. Jung* (Princeton, NJ: Princeton/Bollingen, 1990), paragraph 224.

A

Anima/Animus The archetype that, according to Dr. Beebe's model, carries the mental process that is in the fourth position in the sequence of preferences. In other words, one's fourth process plays a role in personality that reflects the archetypal Anima (feminine) or Animus (masculine). This process usually manifests itself as the opposite gender from the individual. Through the Anima or Animus, we tend to appreciate the characteristics of someone of the opposite gender, sometimes to the point of idealization. As the opposite function and attitude to the first process, it complements the superior function, acting as a backseat driver to remind the dominant of what it is not taking into account. As the gateway to the unconscious, the fourth process provides both intentional access from the conscious to the unconscious and involuntary access from the unconscious to the conscious. Good development of the Anima/Animus process is extremely valuable in providing maturity and balance. This compensating, contrasexual process often appears as something mysterious, compelling, and tantalizingly out of reach. Because this part of ourselves sets up ideals that we may not be able to live up to, we may feel shame and insecurity that we do not operate using this process as we feel we should. This has the benefit, however, of forcing us to recognize the limitations of our capacities.

Archetype A primordial psychic template that facilitates humans' abilities to discern patterns within information in the conscious and unconscious. Archetypes are perceived only indirectly through images and motifs that recur throughout humankind's history and diverse cultures. The nurturing "Earth Mother" and the "Circle of Life" are examples of archetypal images. Jung believed that archetypes are hard-wired into our psyche and that they serve an important purpose in giving direction to human adaptation. Beebe describes eight archetypes that carry the eight processes of everyone's sequence of preferences (appendix B).

Attitude Extraversion (Extraverting), Introversion (Introverting), Perception (Perceiving), and Judgment (Judging). Of the four dichotomies of the type model, the two attitude dichotomies are represented by the first and last letters of the type code. They give information about how we perform our mental operations. These are not mental operations themselves. They are

- The energy focus of Extraverting or Introverting. Each mental process is focused upon and energized by either the objective, external world or our subjective, internal one. The first dichotomy of the code designates the preferred energy focus of our dominant process.
- The orientation to the environment of Judging or Perceiving. By designating the function through which we most prefer to interact with our environment, to Extravert, this fourth dichotomy provides the key that allows our sequence of preferences to be represented by a simple four-letter code.

Auxiliary process (a.k.a. second process) The widely accepted term for the second-most preferred process of a type. The auxiliary process is normally the second to develop and usually becomes the second-most highly developed process. It complements and balances the dominant process in terms of the Perception and Judgment functions and the Extraverting and Introverting attitudes.

C
Complex A constellation of emotionally charged psychic images. Although complexes are thought of, by Jungians, as the basic elements of psychic life and the source of all human emotion, they are not directly incorporated into the type model. The student of type needs to be mindful that the traits and behaviors that can be manifestations of complexes can hide the influences of the innate mental process preferences of type, thus making type interpretation more challenging.

Conflict A state of tension. Conflict is needed to drive personal growth through the development of the mental processes. Conflict can take place internally or externally, within oneself or in relationships, at a conscious or unconscious level.

Conscious That which we are aware of about ourselves. We are born unconscious, and life is a continuing process of becoming conscious. The more we become aware of self and the more effectively we can direct our energy, the more we move into consciousness. Consciousness grows through learning to use the eight mental processes. In normal development, adults have brought their two to four most preferred processes to a level of comfort, familiarity, and control that is considered to be primarily in the realm of the conscious.

- **Collective conscious** The part of the conscious that we hold in common with all humans.
- **Personal conscious** The part of the conscious that is unique to an individual.

D

Demon/Daimon The archetype that, according to Dr. Beebe's model, carries the mental process that is in the eighth position in the sequence of preferences. In other words, one's eighth process plays a role in personality that reflects the archetypal Demon/Daimon. Beebe uses "Demon" when speaking about the destructive, undermining, and negative aspects that are the most common characteristics of the archetype. He uses the Greek term "Daimon" to emphasize the more positive, angelic, and spiritually uplifting aspects. The process in the eighth position usually manifests itself as the same gender as the individual, but as a deeply unconscious process, it can be represented by either gender, by animals, and even by inanimate objects. This is usually the most problematic of all the processes. It almost always operates in a manner that is undermining to others and to oneself. It is capable of gross distortion, causing confusion and chaos and disrupting trust. Most people's concept of Satan and their direct experience of interpersonal "evil" come to them through this process. But, like Lucifer, it can also be the "light bringer," manifesting positive, Daimonic, attributes and effects as well as its more easily recognized Demonic aspects. Like the beast in the fairy tale, this process can be cruel and kind at the same time.

Dichotomy Describes any concept that is split into two mutually exclusive or opposite polarities, like male/female or yin/yang. The four dichotomies of the Myers and Briggs type model are represented by the four letters of the type code. They are the separate but interactive dimensions that define the eight processes and their sixteen possible typological alignments of preferences. They are

- Energy focus: Extraverting and Introverting
- Perception: Sensing and Intuiting
- Judgment: Thinking and Feeling
- External environment focus: Judging and Perceiving

209

Dominant process (a.k.a. first process, Superior). The widely accepted term for the most preferred mental process of a type. Normally, it is the first to develop and becomes the most highly developed process. All other processes can be viewed as working in support of the dominant process.

E

Ego The center of our consciousness. It is who we think of ourselves as being, our identity, the "me." Paradoxically, it is also the me that experiences itself as me. The ego is a product of inherited disposition and acquired impressions. It is the repository of conscious self-knowledge and, as such, an important player in development through individuation.

Eight-process model of type A view of personality type that considers the interactions of all eight Jungian mental processes to be fundamental to the understanding of type theory. The primary benefits of this approach are that it provides a simple and effective methodology for giving feedback and for validation of reported type, while allowing a more direct route to understanding the complexities of type dynamics. Although all of the components of this model have been understood and used by many for years, the authors have never found this approach assembled and explained as a coherent whole. This work is our attempt to fill that gap. Thus, without making any presumptuous claims to be reinventing the wheel, it seems both convenient and appropriate to give this model the label of "eight-process" to distinguish it from ways of thinking about personality type that do not incorporate an awareness of the Jungian processes and the importance of the dynamic nature of the personality system.

Environment In a psychological context, environment means everything outside the psyche. It includes all the information available to the five senses, including perceptions of the body's internal physiology and perhaps also the sixth sense input that many people appear to perceive.

F

Function The two dichotomies that describe the two basic kinds of mental operations that we do according to the type model. These are the two middle letters in the type code. They are
- Perception (taking in information): by Sensing (S) or Intuiting (N)
- Judgment (making decisions): by Thinking (T) or Feeling (F)

H

Hero/Heroine The archetype that, according to Dr. Beebe's model, carries the mental process that is in the first position in the sequence of preferences. In other words, one's first process plays a role in personality that reflects the archetypal Hero (masculine) or Heroine (feminine). This process usually manifests itself as the same gender as the individual. This process is the top authority in our personality, which is why Jung called it our "Superior" function. We place unqualified trust in the process that plays the Hero/Heroine role and depend upon it without reservation. We use this process to take care of ourselves, particularly our ambitions and goals. This is the process that initiates individuation. When we work using of our Hero/Heroine process, our ambition (often realized) is to give a stellar performance in anything we undertake. However, the hero/heroine can think it is the only player in the show and become inflated. After midlife, the Heroic process often seems to become bored with its role and is more willing to defer to other processes.

I

Individuation The bringing of unconscious mental processes into consciousness. The mechanism by which we mature psychologically, through type development.

Instinct The involuntary tendency toward primitive, undeveloped activities that is driven by unconscious energy, particularly in times of stress. Jung said that we have five basic instincts. In order of importance to our survival, beginning with the most important, they are

- Hunger (survival of the individual)
- Sexuality (survival of the species)
- Activity (restlessness)
- Reflection (the search for meaning)
- Creativity (the creative impulse)

M

Mother/Father The archetype that, according to Dr. Beebe's model, carries the mental process that is in the second position in the sequence of preferences. In other words, one's second process plays a role in personality that reflects the archetypal Father or Mother. This archetype is usually the same gender as the individual. Portraying the model of the idealized parent, it functions to take care of others. It is supportive and nurturing and also sets a standard of perfection. It acts as the right hand to the dominant process and is often seen as the older and more mature of the two processes. We need to move to this process to deal with the world. However, it can cause the individual to become an enabler to chronically dependent people, which can end up hurting the caretaker's own psyche.

Myers-Briggs Type Indicator® (MBTI®) A personality inventory that is based on a carefully crafted questionnaire, designed to identify individuals' process preferences. Using a simple formula to represent the preferred mental functions and attitudes, it presents a person with one of sixteen possible process combinations, tentatively identifying how that person innately prefers to operate. This reported type is considered to be a hypothesis of the person's true type. It is then up to the individual to verify his or her true type by getting coaching from type professionals, reading descriptions such as those provided in chapters 4 through 11 of this book, and paying attention to how he or she habitually gathers information and makes choices daily.

O

Opposing Personality The archetype that, according to Dr. Beebe's model, carries the mental process that is in the fifth position in the sequence of preferences. In other words, one's fifth process plays a role in personality that reflects the archetypal Opposing Personality. This archetype is usually associated with a figure or state of mind of the opposite gender from the individual. The fifth process is the first of the four processes (i.e., the processes that occupy the fifth through eighth positions in the sequence) that remain mostly unconscious in normally developed adults. This process often appears oppositional, forcing results that may appear clumsy in contrast to the smooth mastery of the first process. Because the fifth process is the same function as the dominant, but in the opposite attitude, it can seem to speak the same language as the dominant and yet actually be taking a very different, often contradictory approach. Thus the Opposing Personality often serves as an adversary to the Hero/Heroine by criticizing and arguing with him or her. This can have the positive benefit of reminding us that despite our inflated confidence in the dominant process, it can sometimes make mistakes. When out of control, the argument between the Hero/Heroine and the Opposing Personality may become all-consuming. For many of us, clashes with people who prefer our fifth process present our most common interpersonal difficulty. The Opposing Personality uses both passive and aggressive tactics to throw us off balance. It can defend us, though, from the outer world, enabling us to be adversarial and suspicious when appropriate, and to avoid dangerous situations and relationships. This becomes a problem, however, when such defensive reactions are inappropriate.

P

Principle The underlying criterion used in the Introverted Thinking decision-making process. Principles are logical constructs and can therefore be defended, debated, and revised.

Persona The mask that we present to the world. The version of "me" that is created from what we intentionally project as who we are and from what others perceive of us. More often than not, it is an idealized version of ourselves. The persona is created as an adaptation in order to facilitate social interaction because much of our true self is counterproductive to social interaction. The persona is who we, and others, often come to believe we are.

Process (a.k.a. mental process, cognitive process, Jungian mental process, function/attitude). Traditionally used as a synonym for "function." By specifying that we use process only as a shorthand term for the Jungian mental process, the authors are attempting to simplify the terminology. When we say "process," we always mean a function in its specific attitude of Introverting or Extraverting. Thus, the eight processes are

- Extraverted Sensing (Se): Acquisition of objective information through the five senses. Focuses on the environment, here and now.
- Introverted Sensing (Si): Subjective acquisition of information through the five senses. Focuses on inner recall and comparison of past to present.
- Extraverted Intuiting (Ne): Objective perception of the connections associated with information from the environment. Focuses on possibilities and connections.
- Introverted Intuiting (Ni): Subjective abstraction of information from the unconscious and/or environment. Focuses on significance.
- Extraverted Thinking (Te): Objective decision making using logic within a structural organization taken from the environment. Focuses on end results.
- Introverted Thinking (Ti): Subjective decision making using logic within a unique personal framework. Focuses on the process of how the task is accomplished.
- Extraverted Feeling (Fe): Objective decision making using values taken from the environment. Focuses on external harmony.
- Introverted Feeling (Fi): Subjective decision making based on personal core values. Focuses on internal harmony.

Projection The act of seeing and unconsciously reacting to parts of our own unconscious when we see them manifested in others. Projection can cause major conflict. We need to try to be aware when it happens and work to bring it into conscious understanding and control. Beebe's archetypes (appendix B) provide the basis for a concrete approach to understanding and dealing with projection.

Psyche The psychological dimension of an individual taken as a whole. It encompasses all phenomena and activity of our mental life, including our thoughts and emotions, plus their products and manifestations: traits and behavior. It also includes all aspects of personality and the psychic energy system.

Puer/Puella (a.k.a. Puer Aeternus/Puella Aeterna, Eternal Child). The archetype that, according to Dr. Beebe's model, carries the mental process that is in the third position in the sequence of preferences. In other words, one's third process plays a role in personality that reflects the archetypal Puer (masculine) or Puella (feminine). This archetype usually manifests itself as the same gender as the individual, though often with androgynous and unusually charming characteristics. Like a child, it often serves to moderate the purposefulness of the dominant-auxiliary team, enabling the person to "lighten up"— to play, be silly, be creative, and make mistakes. Often seen as a less mature, eager-to-please side of the person, this process has built-in vulnerability and may appear as a wounded child. Dramatic swings in self-confidence can occur here that can take us back and forth between inflation and deflation.

S

Self The archetypal concept of the essence of the individual psyche. It is thought of as both our psychic core that determines our unique psychic nature, while at the same time it encompasses the whole of that personality, including conscious and unconscious, knowable and unknowable. The self is the abstract essence of who we are—of the "me." The ego is its manifestation: the conscious "me" that exists in the world. The persona is the socially acceptable version of "me:" the interface that makes it possible to interact effectively with other humans.

Senex/Witch The archetype that, according to Dr. Beebe's model, carries the mental process that is in the sixth position in the sequence of preferences. In other words, the sixth process plays a role in personality that reflects the archetypal Senex (masculine) or Witch (feminine). This process usually manifests itself as the same gender as the individual. As the second process acts to advise and nurture, the sixth seeks to discourage, cast doubt, and set limits. It often takes a somewhat authoritarian and arbitrary approach. It can be withering. Like any archetypal process, it can carry valuable insights, but its wisdom is usually hard to understand, and at worst it simply gives very bad advice. Often this process attacks the Anima or Animus of someone else. When using a process that is guided by this archetype, one can feel empowered to say no but may be seen as rigid and punitive. Internally, the person can also restrict or depress himself or herself when the Senex or Witch attacks his or her own Anima or Animus, thus paralyzing autonomy, initiative, and self-confidence.

Shadow The poetic term referring to the repressed or unacknowledged aspects of our personality, which are often expressed through our normally unconscious, less preferred mental processes. Since these processes are dynamically positioned to pull us in opposite directions from our preferred processes, and since they usually do so through the primitive and uncontrolled mechanisms available to unconscious processes, they are most often manifested as the negative thoughts, emotions, and behaviors of our "dark side." Their ultimate function, however, is to balance the innate biases of our conscious preferences. Thus, they are also a potential source of tremendous wisdom and creativity. Tapping into this potential is probably what instinctively drives us to push our own type development by exploring our shadow. In normal type development, the fifth through eighth processes in our sequence of preferences remain mostly unconscious in middle-aged adults. Thus, the shadow is sometimes misinterpreted as a label for these four processes as a group. Actually, though, the shadow encompasses all processes that are primarily unconscious in an individual. Which processes these are will depend on that person's type development and can even include all eight in a very young child. Note also that the normal hierarchy of preference for processes five through eight has not yet been empirically established, and in practice is likely to vary from person to person. Beebe cautions us not to assume too much on the basis of his numbering, which in many ways is simply for convenience in identifying the various positions. He simply puts it forth as a tool that he has found useful and informative and which at least for the first four functions seems to reflect the order of conscious cultivation of the functions that he has observed. The numbers for the shadow functions are identified merely to mirror the ordering of the first four.

Stimulus Any input that can be detected by the senses.

T

Trickster (a.k.a. Manipulator, Clown). The archetype that, according to Dr. Beebe's model, carries the mental process that is in the seventh position in the sequence of preferences. In other words, one's seventh process plays a role in personality that reflects the archetypal Trickster. This process usually manifests itself as the same gender as the individual. It can operate very much like a rebellious, mischievous child, tricking and confusing and deviously trying to get its own way. If developed, this process can help us to overcome arbitrary or unreasonable obstacles when it is appropriate and to get out of the double binds that other people set—by putting them in double binds of our own manufacture. Its irreverent approach to life's contradictions may even help us to transcend ourselves to experience the sacred. Beebe believes the Trickster compensates for the vulnerability of the Puer/Puella in us, enabling us to better survive the cruelty of the world. The Trickster also tests limits and frequently brings the wrath of the Senex/Witch in others down upon us.

Type A shorthand term used when talking about the model described in C. G. Jung's theory of personality type and further developed by Katharine Briggs and Isabel Briggs Myers. We also speak of a specific "type" to refer to an individual's preferences among the eight processes. In this use of the term, there are sixteen possible types, as represented by the four-letter personality type code.

Type code A shorthand representation of the functions and attitudes of the type model, which expresses individuals' innate mental process preferences. Each of the sixteen possible types is expressed as a four-letter code. The formula breaks down as follows:

- First letter (Energy): E or I (Extraverting or Introverting)
- Second letter (Perception): S or N (Sensing or Intuiting)
- Third letter (Judgment): T or F (Thinking or Feeling)
- Fourth letter (Environment): P or J (Perceiving or Judging)

Type development The natural development of our individual personality. The process of realization of self. The natural, lifelong process of psychological maturation by becoming familiar with our concious and unconscious mental processes. Increasing familiarity with, comfort with, and ability to intentionally access these processes brings them gradually into the realm of the conscious. (See individuation.) Although the typical sequence and timetable of type development is widely accepted (see appendix C), it is not uncommon for environmental factors to alter the course and outcome of the journey. Type development can also be pursued with conscious intent.

Type dynamics The affects of the inherent dimensions and influences that constitute personality theory. They can be thought of as the forces working within the system of type. These dynamics help to produce our infinitely varied individual personalities from a simple set of coping mechanisms—information gathering and decision making. An understanding of these dynamics is the cornerstone of any true appreciation of the rich insights of type, and is the foundation upon which the eight-process model is built.

U

Unconscious The part of our psyche that includes the personal unconscious and the collective unconscious. Encompassing our less developed processes, it is characterized by the primitive, instinctual forces of the unknown parts of our psyche. The "contents" of the unconscious may or may not ever become conscious. The unconscious is inexhaustible and timeless.

- **collective unconscious** The inherited elements of our psyche that we share with all humans. The spiritual heritage of man's evolution. The source of our ability to know that which would appear to be unknowable. Most often viewed through the abstract symbols and motifs of myths, dreams, and art.
- **personal unconscious** Contains "lost memories"—painful perceptions and ideas that are repressed and forgotten—plus subliminal perceptions that we are not able to take in consciously.

V

Values The underlying criteria used in the decision-making processes Extraverted Feeling and Introverted Feeling. Values are not necessarily logical or defensible. For the Introverted Feeling preference, they are part of one's core being. For Extraverted Feeling, they are adaptations of the values of the culture.

BIBLIOGRAPHY

Beebe, John. *A New Model of Psychological Types.* Audiotape number 317. Chicago: The C. G. Jung Institute of Chicago. 1988.

Beebe, John. "Psychological Types in Transference, Countertransference, and the Therapeutic Interaction." Paper presented at the Chiron Conference, Ghost Ranch, NM. 1983.

Grant, W. Harold, Magdala Thompson, and Thomas E. Clarke. *From Image to Likeness: A Jungian Path in the Gospel Journey.* Mahwah, NJ: Paulist Press, 1983.

Haas, Leona, Robert McAlpine, and Margaret Hartzler. *Journey of Understanding.* Palo Alto, CA: CPP, 2000.

Harris, Anne Singer. *Living With Paradox: An Introduction to Jungian Psychology.* Pacific Grove, CA: Brooks/Cole Publishing Co., 1996.

Hartzler, Margaret and Gary Hartzler. *Functions of Type: Activities to Develop the Eight Jungian Functions.* Huntington Beach, CA: Telos Publications, 2005.

Jung, Carl G. *Psychological Types.* Translated by H. G. Baynes. Revised by R. F. C. Hull. Princeton, NJ: Princeton University Press, 1976.

Jung, Carl G. and M.-L., von Franz, eds. *Man and His Symbols.* Garden City, NY: Doubleday and Co., 1964.

Meisgeier, Charles, and Elizabeth Murphy. *Murphy-Meisgeier Type Indicator for Children: Manual.* Palo Alto, CA: CPP, 1987.

Myers, Isabel Briggs. *Gifts Differing: Understanding Personality Type.* With Peter B. Myers. Palo Alto, CA: Davies-Black, 1995.

Myers, Isabel Briggs, Mary H. McCaulley, Naomi L. Quenk, and Allen L. Hammer, eds. *MBTI® Manual: A Guide to the Development and Use of the Myers-Briggs Type Indicator®.* 3rd ed. Palo Alto, CA: CPP, 1998.

Myers, Katharine and Linda Kirby. *Introduction to Type® Dynamics and Development: Exploring the Next Level of Type.* Palo Alto, CA: CPP. 1994.

Schwartz-Salant, Nathan, and Stein, Murray, eds. *Transference Countertransference.* New York: Chiron Publications, 1984.

Sharp, Daryl. *Personality Types: Jung's Model of Typology.* Toronto: Inner City Books, 1987.

Sharp, Daryl. *C. G. Jung Lexicon: A Primer of Terms and Concepts.* Toronto: Inner City Books, 1991.

Wheatley, Margaret, and Myron Kellner-Rogers. *A Simpler Way.* San Francisco: Berrett-Koehler Publishers, 1999.

Additional Recommended Reading and Tapes

Beebe, John. *Integrity in Depth.* College Station, TX: Texas AandM University Press, 1992.

Beebe, John. "The Peculiar Toolkit of Individuation: John Beebe's Eight Function Model." Presentation before the Vermont chapter of the Association for Psychological Type, Williston, VT, September 9, 2001.

Berens, Linda V. *Dynamics of Personality Type: Understanding and Applying Jung's Cognitive Processes.* Huntington Beach, CA: Telos Publications, 1999.

Berens, Linda V., and Dario Nardi. *Understanding Yourself and Others®: An Introduction to the Personality Type Code.* Huntington Beach, CA: Telos Publications, 2004.

Eliot, Alexander. *The Universal Myths, Heroes, Gods, Tricksters and Others.* New York: Truman Talley Books/Meridian,1990.

Harding, M. Esther. *The I and the Not I.* Princeton, NJ: Princeton University Press, 1993.

Hartzler, Margaret, Robert McAlpine, and Leona Haas. *Introduction to Type® and the Eight Jungian Functions.* Mountain View, CA: CPP, 2005.

Hynes, William J., and William G. Doty, eds. *Mythical Trickster Figures: Contours, Contexts, and Criticisms.* Tuscaloosa: University of Alabama Press, 1997.

Jung, Carl G. 1990. *The Collected Works of C. G. Jung.* Edited by Herbert Read, Michael Fordham, and Gerhardt Adler, executive editor, William McGuire. Vol. 7, *Two Essays on Analytical Psychology.* Translated by R. F. C. Hull. Princeton, NJ: Princeton/Bollingen, 1953.

Jung, C. G. *Memories, Dreams, Reflections.* New York: Random House, 1961.

Jung, C. G. *On the Nature of the Psyche.* Translated by R. F. C. Hull. Princeton, NJ: Princeton/Bollingen, 1960.

Murphy, Elizabeth. *The Developing Child: Using Jungian Type to Understand Children.* Palo Alto, CA: Davies-Black, 1992.

Nardi, Dario. *8 Keys to Self-Leadership: From Awareness to Action.* Huntington Beach, CA: Unite Business Press, 2005.

Saunders, F. W. *Katharine and Isabel: Mother's Light, Daughter's Journey.* Palo Alto, CA: Davies-Black, 1991.

Sharp, Daryl. *Jungian Psychology Unplugged: My Life as an Elephant.* Toronto: Inner City Books, 1998.

Spoto, Angelo. *Jung's Typology in Perspective.* Rev. ed. Wilmette, IL: Chiron Publications, 1995.

INDEX

LEONA HAAS, MS, is a principal of Consultants of the
Future. An accomplished organizational needs assessor and
instructional designer, she is experienced with a multitude
of instruments. Leona has many years' experience coaching
leaders and facilitators in organization change and transition, team development, and conflict management. She has
been coaching executives, conducting team-building off-sites, and using the
MBTI® Step II as a crucial part of her coaching as well as correlating the
MBTI® instrument to the Gallup Strength Finders and various 360-degree
evaluation instruments. Leona has earned an international reputation as a
pioneer in the use of the eight-process model. She has made presentations
at many chapters of the Association of Psychological Type (APT) and at
international conferences on the practical uses of type. She was given the
Innovations in Training and Education Award for the APT XV International Conference. Her workshop "Using the TKI and MBTI® in Conflict
Management," presented in April 2002 to the Chicago chapter of APT, was
awarded the Outstanding Chapter Program for the APT XV International
Conference. She co-authored *Journey of Understanding and Introduction to the
Eight Functions and Type*.

MARK HUNZIKER (INTJ) founded Wellness Re-
sources of Vermont (www.vtwellness.net) to provide coach-
ing and counseling services to individuals and training and
development assistance to organizations. His organizational
development work has encompassed enterprises of all kinds
and sizes, from start-up businesses and nonprofits to giants
such as the New York Times and the U S Department of Homeland Se-

curity. After years of working primarily with teams within organizations, coaching and counseling individuals and couples has become an increasingly important part of his work; enabling him to address people's issues at a more personally transformative level. Mark is a certified personality type Master Practitioner, has a degree in psychology from the University of Vermont and currently serves as Interest Area Consultant in Health and Wellness for the Association for Psychological Type International.

If you would like to share your stories and insights, we would welcome the chance to hear from you. This is a big part of how we learn to better understand the way this all works. You can contact Leona via e-mail at leona@leonahaas.com. Please include your reported type and your level of confidence that it is your true, verified type, as well as your level of experience and/or expertise in the use of the model.

Also, if you are willing to share your story or insights with others, please give us permission to use them in a future publication. All stories and insights will be used anonymously.

We look forward to hearing from you.

CPSIA information can be obtained at www.ICGtesting.com
Printed in the USA
LVOW111311230413

330514LV00005B/254/P